PLANNING A RESEARCH PROJECT

PLANNING A RESEARCH PROJECT

A guide for practitioners and
trainees in the helping professions

MARTIN HERBERT

CASSELL

Cassell Educational Limited
Artillery House
Artillery Row
London SW1P 1RT

Copyright © Martin Herbert 1990

First published 1990

British Library Cataloguing in Publication Data
Herbert, Martin
    Planning a research project: a guide for
    practitioners and trainees in the helping
    professions.
    1. Welfare work. Research. Methodology
    I. Title
    361.3'072

    ISBN 0–304–31850–7
    ISBN 0–304–31846–9 pbk

Designed by Vaughan Allen
Typeset in Linotype 300 Caledonia by Input Typesetting Limited
Printed and bound in Great Britain by Biddles Ltd, Guildford and
King's Lynn

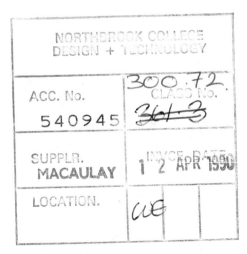

CONTENTS

for Stasia

PREFACE

> Personality is so complex a thing that every legitimate
> method must be employed in its study. Excluded only
> are those fallacious ways that science has long since learned
> to avoid: hearsay, prejudiced observation, impressive
> coincidence, the overweighted single instance, old wives'
> tales, question-begging inductions and deductions, and
> the like.
>
> (Allport, 1937)

Fred Kerlinger, author of a superb book on research, admits that
it is difficult to tell anyone how to do research. Perhaps the best
thing to do, he suggests, is to make sure that the beginner has
a grasp of principles and possibilities; in addition, approaches
and tactics can be suggested. This is the goal of the present
guide. A substantial number of trainees and practitioners in the
helping professions will have experience of doing research; but
many will be newcomers to what is often viewed as an esoteric,
indeed, a daunting activity.

In some ways research activity is not unlike the counselling
or psychotherapeutic process some of you are familiar with. The
same constraints apply as well. Here is Kerlinger again:

> Once the possibilities are known, intuitions can be
> followed and explored. Intuition and imagination,
> however, are not much help if we have little of technical
> resources. On the other hand, good research is not just
> methodology and technique. Intuitive thinking is essential
> because it helps researchers arrive at solutions that are
> not merely conventional and routine. It should never be
> forgotten, however, that analytic thinking *and* creative
> intuitive thinking both depend on knowledge,
> understanding and experience.

I have tried in the following chapters to provide a beginner's
'map' to the *knowledge-base* of the subject. It is of necessity a
large-scale map which, hopefully, will enlarge your *understanding* of the research ethos. For the equivalent fine detail of the
ordnance survey map — statistical formulae, specific techniques

of measurement, etc. — I have listed key references in the Further Reading section. Only you can provide the practical *experience*. There is no substitute for *doing* when it comes to learning statistics or mastering research design and research methods.

The book is divided into two main sections. Part I is concerned with the *planning* of your project and involves identifying a research problem (Chapter 1); choosing a research strategy to address this problem (Chapter 2); and considering the relevance of quantitative or qualitative methods for your purposes (Chapter 3).

Chapter 4 helps you decide on the precise means of assembling your evidence (data), whether it be for exploring an issue or testing a hypothesis. This chapter takes you into the realms of research design, sampling, size of experimental groups, control and so on. In Chapter 5 you will find answers to the *how* questions: how to measure your variables (i.e. the range of methods/tests at your disposal) and how to deal with the important issues of their reliability and validity. Methods such as the interview, questionnaire, direct observation (*inter alia*) are described, with their advantages and disadvantages.

Part II is about the *initiation and implications* of your investigation. Chapter 6 deals with the collection and analysis of evidence. In it I provide a guide to enable you to arrange, analyse and interpret the data. Chapter 7 is about the value and function of a statistical analysis. It deals with applications (*not* formulae) and attempts to persuade those who are apprehensive at the mere mention of the word 'statistics', that they can be user-friendly, helping one to organize, summarize and understand the findings. In Chapter 8 I describe that vital phase of your research in which you draw out your conclusions and then report them. How do you best set out your results and communicate them? Suggestions are offered which I hope will prove useful.

There are five appendices, which deal with: (i) the preparation of a research proposal; (ii) an example of one; (iii) a paper on the ethical acceptability of research with humans; (iv) a guide to assessing research reports; and (v) a guide to a library research. Inevitably there are 'gaps' in an introductory text; most can be filled by further reading. The book ends with an extensive bibliography.

Happy researching!

ACKNOWLEDGEMENTS

I am indebted to Vivienne Doughty for her skill and endurance in typing this manuscript. My gratitude goes to many authors — too many to name — but most particularly Mike Berger, Pauline Hardiker, Derek Jehu and Carolyn Miller for ideas incorporated in this guide.

PART I
Planning Your Research Project

INTRODUCTION

Research has been defined as a process of seeking, by means of methodical enquiry, to solve problems and to add to one's own body of knowledge and that of others by the discovery of significant facts and insights. For clinical psychologists, psychiatrists, medical practitioners and social workers, research is not only about the extension of factual and theoretical knowledge in the field of human problems, but also the application of such knowledge for practical purposes, namely the helping/healing process and policy development.

Types of research

Research can be classified according to its

- *field* (e.g. medical, counselling, brief psychotherapy, rehabilitation);

- *approach* (e.g. exploratory-descriptive, experimental, quasi-experimental);

- *contribution to knowledge*, which can be:
  (a) pure theory;
  (b) testing of existing theory;
  (c) reviews of the 'state of the art';
  (d) finding specific solutions to problems;

- and also, its *purpose* which we now look at.

The purpose of research

There are four common reasons for conducting research:

- to explore (and in the process, describe) and/or resolve some problem;

- to review existing theory and factual knowledge in a particular field;

- to construct something that is useful, for example an instrument to predict the after-effects of anaesthesia on cognitive functioning or to measure stress, or, perhaps, create a questionnaire that reliably indicates patient/client satisfaction with the service they receive;

- to explain or clarify ('unpack') complex phenomena.

Conceptual issues

A major problem with applied research projects, and (in particular) clinical, counselling, educational and other change-orientated psychological research, is that concepts tend to be general, whereas research has to be specific. Berger (1980) illustrates this in the following way, using 'handwriting' as an example:

> Most people in our culture will have a good idea of what is meant by 'handwriting' and for everyday purposes its meaning is not a problem. If, however, you want to study handwriting, or handwriting difficulties, you soon come to appreciate that handwriting is a complex phenomenon in the sense that it has several attributes or dimensions, such as legibility, letter-form, size, speed, spatial properties, slope, density, aesthetic features, and pressure. The ability to write may be dependent on sequencing skills, motor coordination, knowledge of spelling, grammar, the ability to transform mental events into motor sequences, and so on. The concept of 'handwriting', despite its complexity, is comparatively simple when considered in relation to many psychological concepts, such as 'intelligence', 'social skills', 'language', 'adjustment', 'social disadvantage', 'school ethos', 'motivation' and so on.

The researcher needs to capture the essence of the concept when he or she is attempting to measure it in the research project. And therein lies a major difficulty. The concepts are seldom fully specified and even those aspects that are identified necessitate indexing along several dimensions of measurement. The practical implication of all this is that you should be able to answer *clearly* the question 'What do you mean when you use the concept "X"?' and, for that matter, any of the subsidiary ideas and concepts which are mentioned in the preliminary statement of your research problem.

This advice, to be as precise as you can in the conceptual language you use, will apply at every stage described in the flowchart (on page 5) delineating the 'journey' you will have to take as a researcher, but particularly steps 1, 2 and 3.

Pitfalls in human research

What you can (and *must*) count on is that the period between deciding to do some research and getting started is going to be longer than you anticipated — if the job is to be done properly, i.e. meticulously. The research 'journey' is seldom a smooth progression from point A on the map to point B, but one beset — to continue the metaphor — with false starts, culs-de-sac, roadworks and other impediments or diversions.

Theodore Barber, author of *Pitfalls in human research*, lists ten major hazards in research that can directly or indirectly (and he cites the evidence) give rise to misleading results and conclusions (Barber, 1976). In many studies (although seldom in student projects) the investigator and experimenter are not one and the same person(s). The investigator decides that a study is to be conducted, how it is to be designed and carried out, and how it is to be analysed and interpreted. The experimenter is the person who conducts the study, testing/interviewing subjects and, in other ways, collecting data. Misleading results may derive from:

Aspects of the investigator:

- the paradigm used;
- the experimental design;
- the 'looseness' of experimental procedures;
- the analysis of the data;
- the fudging of data.

Aspects of the experimenter:

- his or her personal attributes;
- failure to follow the experimental procedures;
- misrecording data;
- fudging data;
- expectancies (preconceived expectations).

I will touch on these sources of error throughout the book.

Ethical imperatives

At every stage of your research there is a moral or ethical issue to consider. The questions you have to answer include the following:

- Is your client ('subject') making an *informed* and *free* choice in participating in your study?
- Does he or she appreciate all the implications?
- Are your methods ethical?
- Will the individual results be kept confidential?

Check these questions out with colleagues and/or supervisor and, where mandatory, an ethical committee. Familiarize yourself with the many-sided ethical issues inherent in researching into people's bodies, psyches and lives (see Appendix III; also Bulmer, 1982; Gould, 1981).

The process of research

I have drawn up a schematic overview (see opposite) of the processes involved in conducting a modest research project, or (and the basic steps are the same) a more ambitious research programme from inception to conclusion.

FLOWCHART OF RESEARCH PROCESS

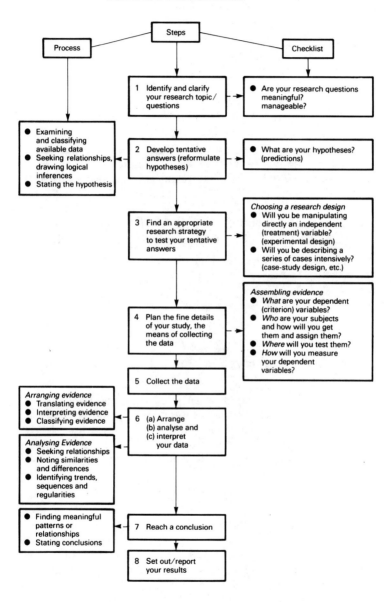

CHAPTER 1

Identifying Problems

This first phase — the one of identifying clearly the problem/s you are setting out to study — seems blindingly obvious, and yet many people fail to work through it with sufficient care. It necessitates asking a series of questions.

STEP 1: IDENTIFY AND CLARIFY YOUR RESEARCH TOPIC) (see Appendix II for an example)

- What is it you wish to find out?
- What is the context of your would-be investigation?
- Why do you wish to investigate this topic?
- What importance does it have either theoretically or practically?
- What (if anything) have other researchers said or done about this issue?

Ask of your research topic: What interesting questions does it raise? List these questions as comprehensively and precisely as you can. 'Fillet' the list until you are left with a few clearly formulated core questions. Without clear, logical (i.e. meaningful) questions you are unlikely to generate useful answers about anything worthwhile.

Literature search

Your questions will direct you to the relevant literature (see Borchardt and Francis, 1986 for a comprehensive guide to the literature on psychology; also Appendix V for medical and other fields of research). You may find it helpful to have a computer search carried out at a university, polytechnic or hospital library, if you have access to one. This will identify the current papers in your area of interest. However, the computer search, if not carefully directed, is a bit of a 'shotgun' approach. It is certainly not a substitute for a more focused, personal search through the abstracts.

Keep a small book handy so that you can keep notes of your questions, ideas and thoughts on the issues and problems which may be salient (see Campbell *et al.*, 1982, on generating research questions). Also keep a detailed record of any reading which may be relevant to the research. A reference-card system should be used from the outset. Notes on the material read can be written on the back of the card. One major advantage of a card-index is that the set of cards, arranged alphabetically by author, can be used for typing up the 'Bibliography' or 'References' section. Below are two typical examples:

> Bebbington, P. E. (1976). 'The effectiveness of Alcoholics Anonymous: The elusiveness of hard data'. British Journal of Psychiatry, 128, 572-580.

> Sutton, C. (1987). A handbook of research for the helping professions. London: Routledge & Kegan Paul.

Prepare a research proposal

As your ideas begin to form, 'bounce' them against as many colleagues as will listen and debate with you. Consult someone who *knows* about the topic. This is a good way of beginning to clarify and refine your *research proposal* (see Appendix I).

By the *end* of this stage, your ideas on the sort of questions you wish to tackle should be sharply defined. Now work out the possible answers.

STEP 2: DEVELOP TENTATIVE ANSWERS

Make a list of your hunches (if you have any), setting down the expected directions in which the answers to your questions might go.

The 'so what?' test

A carefully framed question leads to the kind of 'answers' (explanations) that allow you to test a hypothesis. But is the question worth asking, let alone the bother of answering or (in hypothesis form) testing? Ask yourself: If I get an answer (in one direction or another) to my particular research question and someone says 'so what?', what do I reply? Will I be able to indicate that there *is* a real point (in terms of, say, practical implications, contribution to knowledge and, most particularly, non-triviality) to all my investigative endeavours? A research problem is meaningful to the extent that it addresses some issue that is *theoretically, methodologically* or *technically* relevant.

If you have not been deterred by the 'so what?' test you now transform your question — at least with some research studies — into clearly formulated hypotheses. (Not all investigations are about testing hypotheses!)*

From questions to hypotheses

Hypotheses advance knowledge by helping the researcher to confirm or disconfirm theory. An hypothesis is a limited proposition, being based on a generalization that has not been tested. It is a conjectural statement of the relationship between two or more variables. 'If *X* . . . then *Y*', is a common expression of this association. A *variable* is one of several factors — the *X*s, *Y*s and possibly *Z*s — in an experiment which can be varied, measured or controlled. Good hypotheses:

- are statements about the relationships between variables;

- generate clear implications for testing the stated relationships, i.e. lead to an appropriate research design.

Bakan (1967) has a jaundiced view of experimentation in the field of psychology. Much of it (he claims) falls considerably short of being able to be considered really empirical. He says that an important moment comes early in the psychologist's graduate career when he or she learns that research consists of the testing of hypotheses. Curiosity, interest in the phenomena, or even the complex psychodynamics associated with the getting of hypotheses are brushed aside or, at best, are regarded as 'private processes', about which the least said the better. What the student desperately thinks he or she needs is a testable hypothesis, and it is perfectly all right 'to beg one, or borrow one'.

What testability should, in fact, consist of (according to Bakan) is the enumeration of a set of alternatives. He develops his critique in the following words:

---

* It is wise, if possible, to arrange for a research supervisor (or consultant), especially if you are a novice at research. Research is something we should all do — however modest in scope — and I do not wish to discourage anyone! But it can be a bit of a minefield for the newcomer; so a guide (even on a one-off or occasional basis) should be considered. In the case of student projects, supervision is, of course, formally arranged.

Consider the ideal of the well-designed experiment. The usual meaning of 'well designed' is that the outcomes of the experiment have been completely anticipated and that one will not allow the experience of conducting the experiment to lead one to consider alternatives outside of the one already thought of beforehand . . . I must qualify. There is nothing intrinsically wrong with testing hypotheses. It is an important part of the total investigatory enterprise. What I do wish to point out, however, is that by the time the investigatory enterprise has reached the stage of testing hypotheses, most of the important work, if there has been any, has already been done. . . The main work of the scientist is thinking and making discoveries of what was not thought of beforehand. Psychologists often attempt to 'play scientist' by avoiding the main work.

Let us follow up Bakan's point by looking at the source of ideas and hypotheses.

INTERLUDE

The development of testable hypotheses flows from the individual's speculations, consideration and evaluation of the work of others (examining and classifying available information). Particularly important are the insistent, recurring questions that arise from your observations and/or practice. The issue of how ideas and knowledge are acquired is important enough to justify a digression.

Personal experience and common sense

The knowledge a clinical (or social work) practitioner/trainee uses may derive from his or her own personal experience. For example, they may find that a particular intervention is successful with a particular kind of personal problem.

Unfortunately, there are many hazards in relying on personal experience. The observation and recording of what is experienced may be unreliable. Generalizations may be formed on the basis of inadequate evidence. Evidence may be distorted by personal biases or neglected because it does not accord with previous experience. The salient features of a situation may not be distinguished from those which were irrelevant. Causal inferences may be incorrectly or prematurely drawn.

Of course, common-sense 'theories' must not be denigrated. A common-sense view of what the world is like, and how people are likely to react to us, serves most of us fairly well in our day-to-day life. But there are different levels of understanding (and of explanation) when behaviour is investigated.

Kay (1978) has this to say:

> I am a great believer in commonsense, in relying on the good sense of mankind to 'get it right'. It generally does in the end. But the fact that commonsense may have had it wrong for a few preceding millennia does mean that we need to be on our guard and not be too hasty over the certainty of any answers. For example, at one time everybody knew we lived on a flat world; it was self-evident until someone went to the edge and did not fall off. About the same time, everyone knew that the sun charioted around the earth each day, whilst the earth was the centre of the universe, and so on. As we have come to accept, blood has to be spilt before commonsense accepts change, but eventually it does and yesterday's hearsay becomes today's credo, whilst commonsense forgets that it was ever otherwise.

A psychologist would usually wish to understand the processes which precede certain behavioural outcomes to the extent that he or she is able to make accurate predictions on the basis of such knowledge. This is a more precise and technical level of explanation than the 'Aha! Now I've got it' level of understanding most of us are satisfied with in everyday life. The objective of studying behaviour, systematically and scientifically, is to produce understanding, prediction and control above the levels achieved by unaided common sense.

The questions 'what?' 'why?' and 'how?' are the ones professionals ask in their quest for an understanding of behaviour and in their attempt to assess (and remedy) problems. Our everyday answers to questions, our common-sense understanding, are made up of some facts, many fallacies and even more misconceptions. Let us look at one of the ways misunderstandings arise. The observation or finding of a correlation (association) between events is often interpreted as meaning a causal relationship. But a correlation does not necessarily imply causation. The fallacy, an ancient one referred to as 'post hoc ergo propter hoc', has a tendency to crop up frequently in statistical material. It is the one that says that if B follows A, then A has caused B. An unwarranted assumption is being made that since A (say depression) and B (say alcohol) go together, A causes B; i.e. depression leads to alcoholism. Couldn't it just as well be the other way around? Perhaps B leads to A, i.e. heavy drinking causes depression. But then some might say that it is a good deal more probable that neither of these things had produced the other in a simple manner, but both are the product of some third factor. Can it be that the sort of person who is *vulnerable to life stress* and to depressive reactions is also likely to drink more? Maybe vulnerable people use drink as a general means of coping with stress. The point is that when there are many reasonable explanations we are hardly entitled to pick one that suits our taste and insist on it (see Huff, 1954).

Huff makes the point that to avoid falling for the post hoc fallacy you need to put any statement of relationship through a sharp inspection. The correlation can actually be any of several types:

- The correlation produced by chance. You may be able to get together a set of figures or prove some unlikely thing in this way, but if you try again your next set may not prove it at all.

- The correlation in which the relationship is real but it is not possible to be sure which of the variables is the cause and which the effect. In some of these instances cause and effect may change places from time to time, or indeed both may be cause and effect at the same time. A correlation between income and ownership of stocks might be of that kind. The more money you make, the more stock you buy, and the more stock you buy, the more income you get.

Authority

Another way of finding out is to ask another person or consult his or her writings. Indeed, this method — consulting the literature — has already been recommended to you. The success of this approach depends upon the question being well phrased so that it is understood; likewise the answer. It also depends upon the questioner choosing an authority who knows the answer and has good evidence to back it up.

The main problem with this approach is that a critical evaluation of answers can only be attempted where several authorities can be approached. Several reassuringly similar answers from people with authority should not mislead us into believing that a consensus guarantees 'truth'.

Deductive reasoning

Deductive reasoning, often in syllogistic form, has been an important method of acquiring knowledge since the teaching of Socrates, Plato and Aristotle. The syllogism consists of three statements, of which the first two are the premises or evidence for the third statement which concludes the argument.

People with personal problems can be helped by
counsellors. This person has a personal problem.
Therefore she can be helped by a counsellor.

Jehu (1972) notes that the syllogism only enables us to deduce
the consequences of what was already known. Thus, while it
permits logical deductions from known facts, it does not yield
any really new knowledge. Furthermore, if one of the premises
is untrue then the conclusion will be false.

In the example it may be that there are people with personal
problems who cannot be helped by counsellors, or that the
person concerned does not have a personal problem; in either
case the conclusion will not be valid.

While deduction is a useful tool for obtaining certain kinds of
information, it must not be relied upon exclusively. The truth of
the premises must be examined, and the limitations of deduction
in respect of the extension of new knowledge clearly recognized.

Empiricism and inductive reasoning

Empirical knowledge about the world is regarded by many as
the most trustworthy form of knowledge. It may arise in many
ways, but there are extreme and contrasting possibilities. At one
extreme is intuitive belief. This will be asserted by an individual
as his or her view about an aspect of the world. It may be
grounded on personal experiences, or it may be a belief based
only on other people's stories of their experiences — most likely
some vague blend of both.

Intuitive belief contributes to our views about the world not
only as the basis of 'common sense' but also playing an important
role in the work of professional scientists. An important problem
with intuitive belief is that it may be mistaken. The child, limited
by its narrow experience, may over-generalize and identify (say)
all cats as the family pet. Likewise, our own experiences of the
world, even as adults, can be limited; and our knowledge of it
may be biased as well as incomplete. The stereotyping in racial,
sexist and other forms of prejudice typify these problems.

Another alternative form of empirical knowledge is scientific-
based empiricism. The empirical approach to knowledge con-
tends that the sole criterion for judging a statement of fact is
whether or not it coincides with our observations. If it does, it
is accepted; if not, it is repudiated. Sir Francis Bacon (1561–1626)
maintained that one should, by careful observation, collect one's
own data and use these as a basis for making generalizations.

This reference of questions to the world to which they refer
is the essence of empiricism. It is the foundation upon which all

science is based. There are several risks (in addition to the ones mentioned at the beginning of this guide) in using this criterion alone:

- After all, there is abundant psychological evidence that observations may be distorted by the motivation, memory or previous experience of the observer. Tall people overestimate the height of others, fat people their weight and neurotic individuals their neurosis.

- Then again, there is the problem of sampling. It is rarely possible to observe all instances of a phenomenon, i.e. one cannot often ascertain the incidence of a particular problem in a community by interviewing every person in the community.

Instead one might interview a sample of people from the community and then infer the incidence of the problem in the whole community from its incidence in the sample. The soundness of this inference is influenced by the size and representativeness of the sample on which it is based. What we have here is inductive reasoning from a sample; it does not necessarily give the truth. Rather it yields conclusions which are true in varying degrees of probability. Generalizations about the problematic ('storm and stress') nature of adolescence extrapolated from the jaundiced writings of psychiatrists who, by definition, only tend to see difficult or disturbed teenagers, is a good example of the dangers of biased sampling (see Herbert, 1987b).

Having heeded the earlier cautionary note about the dangers of inductive post hoc reasoning (i.e. its logical problems) it is worth remembering that it *is* very nearly the life-blood of science. The more often we can show that situation Y is associated with consequence Z, the more confident we can be that there are factors inherent in situation Y which at least contribute to Z. It is the beginning of precise hypothesis testing. And the word 'precise' is important because it is only too easy to 'find' causes for anything one likes. Post hoc reasoning provides a hunch which is the first stage in formulating a hypothesis for testing. Empiricism and inductive reasoning do generate new knowledge, whereas deductive reasoning is restricted to the knowledge already stated in the premises. These lead us to what has proved a most fruitful means of acquiring knowledge in the physical and psychological disciplines, although the limitations of scientific enquiry into the latter are increasingly acknowledged.

Scientific research

Science has as its principal aim the description of the world in sufficient detail that at least it will be possible to predict its 'behaviour'. The physical sciences were the first to break away from natural philosophy as a methodology developed that allowed empirical questions to be posed. In the process, the disciplines of chemistry and physics were born.

We have contrasted inductive methods with deductive methods. The former were characterized by the relatively unselective collection of data from which generalizations could emerge later. Until about the sixteenth century, scholars had still to develop a method of making and selecting their observations so that they yielded coherent, reliable and significant knowledge.

From around the seventeenth century, Isaac Newton (1642–1727) and others made use of a synthesis of observation and reasoning in a method now frequently used in scientific research. It is possible to consider this method as consisting of five stages:

1. The first stage is the formulation of the question to be answered in the research. It has been said that the art of scientific investigation is to ask the right question. The right question is one that leads to useful answers — answers that add to knowledge.

2. Having formulated an appropriate question, the next stage in scientific research is the collection of relevant observations.

3. In the third stage, the researcher formulates a hypothesis to explain the relationships between the observed facts.

4. Next he or she works out the observable consequences of the hypothesis if it is true.

5. And finally, he or she enters the cycle of enquiry again by attempting to verify their hypotheses by making more observations to see if they conform to their predictions.

This sequence is called the *hypothetico-deductive method*. It emphasizes the explicit development of a model from which a hypothesis is developed and observations then planned to test it.

Not a few scientists have challenged the pragmatic value of this analysis, since it is almost impossible to contemplate collecting data without some degree of selection; likewise, the source of the hypotheses tested in the deductive process cannot be left unspecified. In fact, science in the real world makes progress in a much more untidy way than philosophers of science would seem to suggest.

We have a situation in which knowledge grows by a series of successive approximations and adjustments in the light of new findings, partly because there is no known path which will lead inexorably to the truth in any domain.

Jehu (1972) stresses the important reservation that, although the scientific method is a very valuable way of acquiring new knowledge, it should be recognized that:

- it does not yield absolute or eternal truth, but rather systematic doubt; it reduces uncertainty rather than producing absolute knowledge. And it cannot answer questions involving moral or value-judgements, only questions of a factual nature.

The scientific researcher may shift frequently between collecting information, putting forward hypotheses to explain his or her data, working out the logical consequences of hypotheses and obtaining more data for their validity. This method of acquiring knowledge encourages doubt and further investigation until evidence is obtained which is consonant with the hypotheses advanced. Moreover, if fresh evidence arises at a later date which is no longer congruent with the deduced consequences of a particular hypothesis, that hypothesis must be modified or abandoned. In this way, science contains a *self-corrective* mechanism.

Sadly, the helping professions are not always good at modifying cherished theories and practices on the basis of contradictory evidence or of 'putting down' sacred cows when their time has come.

CHAPTER 2

Deciding on Your Research Strategy

Ideas into operations

Before you can think through the details of your research design you must translate your ideas into potential 'operations'. An operational definition assigns explicitness to a concept (construct or variable) by specifying the publicly observable activities or 'operations' necessary to measure/manipulate it. It is, to quote Kerlinger (1986), 'a sort of manual of instructions to the investigator'. Berger's helpful guide to student dissertations emphasizes the importance of the way in which the ideas are translated into operations. These operations include the selection of the research design, the methods, sampling and implementation procedures, data gathering and analysis. Each of these is the subject of whole textbooks (see Technical References and Further Reading).

Try to ensure that the appropriate operations are applied to meet your particular research problem. Berger (1980) illustrates this by the following example:

> You may be interested for various reasons in the personality characteristics of Down's syndrome children and would like at the end of the study to be able to make certain statements about their personality. Do you want to be able to generalize about all Down's children, only males, within a narrow chronological age band or only males whose chronological and mental ages are not grossly discrepant, or do you want to know about children from middle-class families? That is, children with Down's syndrome vary in sex, age, abilities, accompanying handicaps and come from a variety of backgrounds. Before you begin work you have to select a group defined in such a way that the results enable you to draw conclusions which both reflect your concerns and which are valid.

> You cannot, for example, talk about Down's children
> *generally* if you have not selected a representative
> random sample or at least a very large random sample.

The tasks required of you do not end here. You now have
to choose some way of assessing personality. There are varied
definitions of personality and a multitude of tests to enable you
to identify and quantify certain characteristics. Which of these
should you choose? Berger's answer is:

> If you are trying to show that personality in Down's
> syndrome is less diverse than in non-Down's children,
> you have to choose a procedure which gives you a good
> chance of optimizing individual differences, and ensure
> that the test is psychometrically and psychologically
> respectable. At the same time it has to be one which can
> be used with Down's and non-Down's children and so on.

The goal of both basic and applied research is to produce data
that are accurate, generalizable and valid. Judd and Kenny (1981)
take up the vital issue of validity, describing four aspects:

1. Construct validity: this indicates the extent to which
    the theoretical constructs of treatment, outcome,
    population and setting have been successfully
    operationalized.
2. Statistical conclusion validity: this is the extent to
    which the research design is sufficiently precise or
    powerful for us to detect effects on the measured
    outcome, should they exist.
3. Internal validity: this refers to the extent to which the
    detected effects on the outcome are due to the
    operationalized treatment rather than to other possible
    competing causes.
4. External validity: here we are indicating the extent to
    which the effects we observe among operationalized
    constructs can be generalized to theoretical constructs
    other than those specified in the original research
    hypothesis.

The authors make the point that construct validity refers to the
relationships between theoretical constructs and their operations. Both conclusion and internal validity refer to the relationship between the carefully specified and measured treatment
and the defined and measured outcome. Internal validity is concerned with whether that relationship is a causal one. External
validity concerns the relationship between the hypothesized

constructs that were operationalized and other constructs of interest that were not.

The words operations and operational, mentioned above, will recur in successive chapters as they play such an important part in the process of deciding on your research strategy.

STEP 3: DECIDE ON AN APPROPRIATE RESEARCH STRATEGY

By now (hopefully) you are in a position to think about selecting your broad research design. The main criteria of a research design can be summed up in two questions: Does the design generate answers to the research question? Does it adequately test the hypotheses if it is a hypothesis-testing study? The key to success is to plan in advance and ensure that the projected analysis *is* of a logical type which will enable you to answer the research problem. But do not let the analysis dictate or restrict your research completely. There are usually different ways of analysing results and you need to select procedures which help answer the question being posed in a non-simplistic and meaningful manner (see the Technical Bibliography near the end of the book).

Unfortunately there is a tendency for would-be researchers in the helping professions to suffer from 'tunnel vision' when considering strategies for answering research questions. This restricted view may be due to the absence of research experience and training, or (where there has been some training) the result of an undergraduate course that focused on particular methods, such as laboratory experiments. The crucial point to remember is that the research problem or question should determine the approach. There are several approaches — they are not necessarily mutually exclusive — to select from:

Library research

The approaches to student research dissertations are most commonly *empirical* in the sense that you go out and, in one way or another, collect information and data pertinent to answering your research questions. It is also research to collect ideas, theories and reported empirical data, within the context of scholarship in the library — analysing and integrating your findings to illustrate and clarify (indeed revise or reject) an established conceptual framework or theoretical model/perspective (see Herbert, 1964; Herbert *et al.*, 1983).

Problem-solving research

This is often the starting point for people in the helping professions: a problem in the 'real world' of practice. The problem has to be described and defined, and a solution sought (see Sutton, 1987).

Exploratory research

Here you are tackling a novel problem about which little is known. So the major purpose of exploratory research is the development and clarification of ideas, and the formulation of questions and hypotheses, for more precise subsequent investigation. The emphasis is not necessarily on quantitative description or on the establishment of cause–effect relationships. Therefore representative sampling and experimental rigour may be of less importance (although certainly not insignificant) than is the selection of cases to stimulate and clarify ideas. Typically, exploratory studies include much information about a single case or a small number of cases (Allport, 1937).

Descriptive research

Descriptive studies have a range of objectives:

- Describing certain characteristics of populations. Population studies aim to provide accurate quantitative information about certain designated characteristics of a population. These may take the form of social surveys. Example: how many people in a community have certain problems or needs?

- Seeking relationships between variables. Relationship studies aim to determine whether there are any significant correlations between certain variables. Example: is there a correlation between examination fears and personality type?

These studies simply ascertain the existence of an association between variables, not its causation.

Experimental research

The best way to establish the validity of *causal* theories is to test them experimentally. To establish (for example) that a drug treatment is responsible for a particular effect, the medical experimenter needs to establish a situation in which he or she can demonstrate that the treatment precedes the effect, that the effect follows the introduction of the treatment, and that nothing but the treatment (the drug) is responsible for that effect.

In a physics experiment one would show that a physical factor X *caused* a reaction of a particular kind (the effect Y) by keeping everything except X constant, systematically varying X, and observing and measuring changes in the 'behaviour' of Y.

In an experiment on drug effects in human beings (leaving aside for the moment the all-important ethical implications), the ideal situation for a demonstration of the efficacy of a drug (i.e. its causal relationship to the eradication of a disease process) would be to find two identical groups of patients with the identical disease, treat them identically except that only one group receives the drug treatment, test them under identical conditions, and then compare the fate of the disease in the two groups. Now clearly the experimenter simply cannot reproduce such 'perfect' conditions.

What are the implications for clinical, social and psychological research, where it would be very unusual to find identical groups and impossible to test subjects under truly identical conditions? It means that, at best, you have to find a *rigorous* compromise. If you find a difference between your treatment and no-treatment groups, you have to acknowledge the possibility that this difference may be due to non-treatment factors. The rigorous element referred to above is your effort to reduce the possibility as much as is feasible. The non-treated group (to take one example) would have to *believe* that it had received the treatment. The use of chemically inert placebos to induce this belief raises awesome ethical issues.

Independent versus dependent variables

Researchers are likely to be interested (*inter alia*) in determining the relationships between variables of behaviour. The test of a theory or hypothesis is what happens to the so-called 'dependent variables' when we manipulate the 'independent variables'.

An independent variable is the presumed cause of the dependent variable, the presumed effect. The independent variable is the antecedent; the dependent variable is the consequent (thus, if X then Y).

What choices do we have? There are:

- laboratory experiments (in medical research animal subjects are frequently used); and

- natural (field) experiments referred to earlier. These are experiments conducted in natural/realistic surroundings and circumstances, e.g. testing a hypothesis about parent training programmes and their relationship to more effective and enjoyable child management. They cover a variety of designs (see below).

Common to all these experimental designs is the general strategy of holding constant *all* (it is hoped) factors except the independent variable under investigation. Where these cannot be controlled directly, some form of statistical control, involving the distribution or balancing of these confounding factors (e.g. by randomization) between conditions, is put into effect. Such an approach is obviously potent as it permits any differences between experimental and control conditions to be attributed with some confidence to the only variable that was allowed to vary systematically.

In experiments, the independent variable is the variable manipulated by the researcher. When, for example, counselling researchers investigate the effects of different counselling methods, they may manipulate the *method* — the independent variable — by using different counselling methods or approaches (e.g. non-directive, behavioural, psychodynamic counselling). The dependent variable would be some measure of the effect on the client's well-being.

In the field of psychology and (more often than not) in the clinical domain, the concern of researchers is likely to be with *multiple* relationships — several causal factors. Because social-psychological causes do not work *singly*, each cause would, in theory, require a new experimental group each time, thus necessitating a substantial number of subjects (see page 44). For example, favourable outcomes in counselling or brief psychotherapy are complex, including client variables, counsellor variables, seriousness of problems, time factors, training/experience and so on. But this is not all. Variables like these *interact*; they work with each other, sometimes against each other, mostly in uncertain ways, to affect therapeutic outcomes.

While it is possible to run an experiment in which several 'treatments' or 'conditions' are put into effect simultaneously (see page 44), several groups would have to be found, necessitating the range and number of subjects seldom available at any one time or in any one location. Such a project would not be practicable for most researchers, whose resources are modest. Fortunately there are experimental designs utilizing powerful statistical methods available to analyse what are referred to as multivariate problems (see Kerlinger, 1986). I will return to these designs in Chapter 4.

The laboratory experiment (as such), while invaluable for much medical research, is not always seen to be relevant to psychotherapists, counsellors or others working in the areas of the academic humanities or humanistic therapies. Field (*in situ*) experiments are more likely to be pertinent. Studies conducted in non-laboratory conditions, but subjected to certain controls, are the bread and butter of clinical, counselling and social work research. As hypothesis-testing investigations they represent a point of transition between other forms of descriptive research and experimental work of the more direct kind. They are therefore often referred to as 'quasi-experiments'.

Quasi-experimental research

'True' experimental designs — for various reasons to do with ethics, small numbers, the difficulties of randomizing — are not always possible in the 'real world' of social and health service provision. Quasi-experiments have thus proved to be useful in a clinical and educational context (Cook and Campbell, 1979). In this approach there is a reliance on 'natural experiments' (e.g. studying ex-post facto the effects of psychodynamic life events or physical factors like smoking) and 'single case' studies. Pre–post (before and after intervention) designs are useful in evaluating therapies and other service delivery systems. These designs (elaborated below) can be applied to individual cases, units or whole organizational systems.

Descriptive studies of a hypothesis-testing kind differ from true experiments in that the former *typically* do not include randomization procedures or the manipulation of independent variables. The researcher does not have direct control over independent variables because their manifestations have already occurred or because they are inherently not manipulable (see Lee and Herbert, 1970; Toch, 1969). Inferences about relationships among variables are made from a past (assumed) variation of independent and dependent variables. The independent variable is the variable that 'logically' has some effect on a dependent variable. For example, in the research on cigarette smoking and lung cancer, smoking cigarettes (which *has already taken place* among so many people, is the independent variable — the presumed cause). The dependent variable is lung cancer — the hypothesized effect.

Jehu (1972) states that if one wanted to investigate the causation of a relationship between the degree of permissiveness in a children's home and the amount of problem behaviour exhibited by the children:

- One could conduct a descriptive study of identifying groups of children in homes of varying degrees of permissiveness and then compare these contrast groups in respect of the amount of problem behaviour exhibited by them.

- Alternatively, experimentally, one could randomly allocate children to groups, and then randomly allocate these groups to regimes of varying permissiveness which have been arranged for. Pre- and post-treatment measures of problem behaviour would be required: the former to check that on average the groups are roughly equal, the latter to pick up differences due to variations in regime.

Single case ($N = 1$) designs (see Kazdin, 1982)

This research strategy lends itself particularly, but not exclusively, to behaviour therapy/modification and skills training, where it is usual for goals to be explicitly specified. It allows you:

- to assess changes in the client over time;
- to demonstrate a link between these changes (dependent variables) and particular therapeutic or training regimes (independent variables);
- to maximize the opportunity for innovation and flexibility in the intervention, while laying the basis for the formulation and testing of hypotheses.

Barlow *et al.* (1984) provide guidelines and steps for using measurements of change in the individual client:

- State the client's problems in specific terms.
- Specify the several problem areas.
- Obtain multiple measures for each problem behaviour.
- Select measures that are both sensitive and meaningful.
- Collect measures early in the course of treatment.
- Take the same measures repeatedly, at least before, during and after treatment.
- Make comparisons within measures only if the data are collected under similar conditions.
- Graph the data.
- Record inconvenient measures less frequently than convenient ones.
- Select measures with appropriate psychometric properties,

looking for certain types of reliability such as inter-judge agreement, and noting that some types of reliability are less appropriate. For example, test–retest reliability presupposes consistency, but usually the therapist needs a measure of change.

The pre-interventive record is known as a baseline and is useful in defining the problem and (by comparison with the termination record) indicating progress or lack of it. Baseline (and other pre-intervention assessments) thus provide a *standard* against which to measure change. The manner in which the therapeutic interventions are systematically varied directly affects the conclusions that can be drawn from the manipulation. Three examples follow:

(a) AB and ABC designs

These are the simplest of the *time series* single-case designs. Symbol A represents a baseline during which the problem is monitored under uncontrolled conditions, and the symbols B, C, D, etc., represent different treatment programmes (or strategies) or additional inputs (say practical support). The experimental AB design in Figure 1(a) and the ABC design in Figure 1(b) involve a comparison of baseline measures with measures obtained in one or two interventions, respectively.

(b) Reversal designs

The reversal or (ABAB) design (see Figure 2) has a characteristic form; the baseline performance is measured first and identified as the A phase. Next the independent variable (say, behavioural intervention) is introduced. This is the B phase. Then the independent variable is removed. The return to baseline conditions when the independent variable is temporarily removed is frequently referred to as the reversal or the probe. Because these conditions are allegedly 'identical' with the baseline conditions, the phase is also labelled A. The independent variable is once more introduced. This reintroduction of the treatment condition is again labelled B. You will see how the reversal design comes to be referred to as an ABAB design. If, during the third stage, when the intervention is discontinued, the target behaviour does indeed approximate to the original baseline level, then you have support for the notion that the problematic behaviour would have persisted without treatment. The fourth stage should be followed by another reduction in the deviant behaviour. If such a result is obtained it is a reasonable (but by no means certain) assumption that it is the intervention which is producing the change in behaviour. What this kind of design yields is essentially

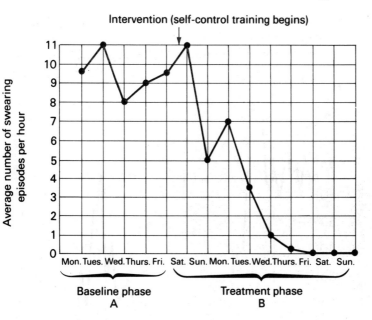

Figure 1(a). Frequency of swearing episodes before and after a behavioural intervention (this is an imaginary record to illustrate an AB research design)

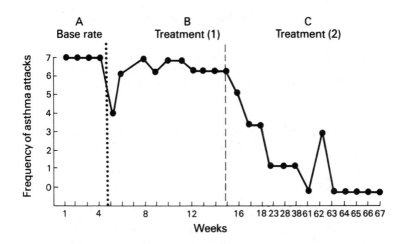

Figure 1(b). Frequency of asthma attacks prior to, during and following (1) cognitive therapy and (2) training in relaxation (this is an imaginary record to illustrate an ABC research design)

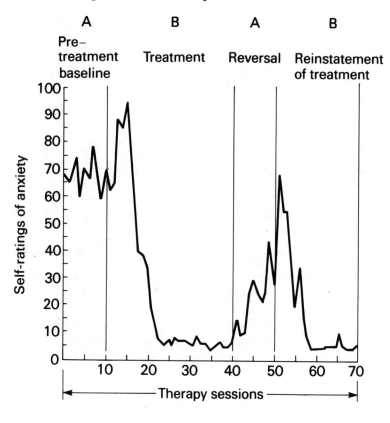

Figure 2. Changes in self-ratings anxiety as a function of the
application and withdrawal of treatment (this is an imaginary
record to illustrate the ABAB research design)

correlational evidence of an association between a treatment and
a reduction in problem behaviour.

(c) Multiple-baseline designs

Multiple-baseline designs (Kazdin, 1982) involve comparing and
contrasting change in those behaviours which have been treated
with other behaviours which have not been treated. For example, a child who manifests three relatively discrete behaviour
problems such as aggressiveness, oppositional behaviour and
extreme attention-seeking might be treated specifically for the
oppositional behaviour and extreme attention-seeking; changes

in respect to these behaviours can then be compared with fluctuations in the problem which has been left untreated.

If, however, only one category of problem (say aggression) was involved, the same treatment is applied in sequence to several baselines for different forms of aggressive behaviour. Alternatively, an intervention can be made across a number of behaviours, but in only one of several settings, while the behaviour is monitored in all the settings. For an example of the design across children being treated for shyness see Figure 3.

Designs of this type, then, determine whether a change in the level of the 'problems' or 'skills' has occurred, and the approximate magnitude of that change. The client's self-report and behaviour are recorded, with the resultant scores (counts, or ratings) plotted graphically. Do remember that some clients change during the baseline recording.

There are other designs you might consider in monitoring specific behaviours/problems:

- the alternative treatments design (Barlow and Hayes, 1979);

- the changing criterion design (Kazdin, 1982).

Inferences about causation require great caution, particularly in the case of the AB design. Several statistical methods of analysing single-case data have been employed (see Kazdin, 1982).

Field studies (see Whyte, 1981)

These are non-experimental scientific enquiries aimed at discovering the relationships and interactions among psychological, educational and sociological variables within social structures (e.g. agencies, schools, hospitals, communities). These studies can be exploratory in nature, or concerned with hypothesis testing.

Epidemiological research

This may be retrospective, prospective or cross-sectional in design and is of particular value in the physical and mental health fields. Epidemiology is concerned with population rates of illness and also with detecting factors which are associated with their origin, course and outcome (see Leighton, 1979). Research obviously has important implications for our understanding of diseases and disorders, and also for the planning of health services — identifying, as it does, prevalence rates and level of need in the community (see Brown and Harris, 1978).

It has been said that surveys are helpful in answering the 'what?', 'when?', 'how?' and 'where?' questions, but not too good

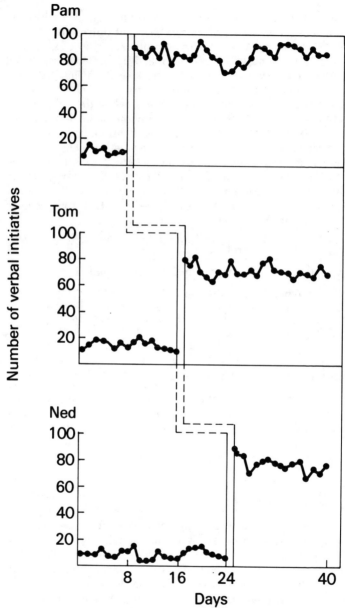

Figure 3. Daily count of verbal initiatives for Pam, Tom and
Ned monitored across experimental speech therapy
conditions (an imaginary record for illustrative purposes).
This is a multiple baseline research design showing the
baseline measures prior to treatment; the application of
treatment; and measures at the end of treatment

on the 'why?' question. Causal relationships do not lend themselves to proof by survey methods.

Surveys range from what are hoped to be 100 per cent population figures to data based upon small but (again hopefully) *representative* samples of a given population. All respondents are asked to answer the same questions, by postal questionnaire, telephone enquiry or direct, i.e. face-to-face, interview. You can imagine how difficult it is to convey identical meaning to people by the use of questions; so, much skill is required in the wording of questions.

Panels of (say) consumers may be surveyed about their opinions and attitudes in a less structured manner, by means of personal interviews, group discussions, and so forth. Methods include:

- case–control studies: for example, cases' (e.g. abusive parents) exposure to risk (say, high alcohol intake) as compared with that for control subjects;

- cohort studies: here subjects are grouped according to whether they have been exposed to the putative cause (say, heavy drinking) and are compared in terms of relative frequency (of, say, child abuse) with those who are not heavy drinkers.

It would also be possible to obtain a representative sample of a population and divide it into cases (child abusers) and non-cases (not-abusive parents) using standardized techniques. In both variants it should be possible to assess the importance of any risk factor (see Mausner and Kramer, 1985 for a discussion of epidemiology).

Action research (see Brown and McIntyre, 1981)

This involves the carefully documented (and monitored) study of an attempt by you and/or your team to actively solve a problem and/or change a situation (see references to 'Participant observation' in the Technical Bibliography — 'Methods' section). It will be seen from a description of the problem-solving features of action research provided below by Brown and McIntyre (1981) that it lends itself to research into clinical programmes, community projects and educational curriculum development.

They state that the research questions arise from:

> . . . an analysis of the problems of the practitioners in the situation and the immediate aim then becomes that of understanding those problems. The researcher/actor, at an early stage, formulates speculative, tentative general

principles in relation to the problems that have been identified; from these principles, hypotheses may then be generated about what action is likely to lead to the desired improvements in practice. Such action will then be tried out and data on its effects collected; these data are used to revise the earlier hypotheses and identify more appropriate action that reflects a modification of the general principles. Collection of data on the effects of this new action may then generate further hypotheses and modified principles, and so on as we move towards a greater understanding and improvement of practice.

Evaluative research (see Judd and Kenny, 1981)

This is the attempt to assess the effects of interventions, and for clinical purposes, particular therapeutic or rehabilitation *methods*. It is also about the analysis of counselling, psychiatric and social casework and psychotherapeutic *processes* so as to further our understanding of 'therapeutic ingredients' and thus fit the most appropriate treatment method to the particular client or problem.

A classic review of counselling effectiveness is that of Truax and Carkhuff (1967). Here are two more examples of topics studied:

- The comparative effectiveness of paraprofessionals, such as community volunteeers, and professionals, in helping some groups of people with their difficulties in living (Durlak, 1979).

- The usefulness of bereavement counselling (Parkes, 1980).

The basic evaluation model, as defined by Judd and Kenny (1981), is:

> . . . one in which persons or other units that the program is expected to affect have been assigned to levels of the treatment (including, perhaps, no treatment) and subsequently some outcome variable or variables are measured that are expected to show the impact of treatment.

There are various routes to choose from in the evaluation exercise:

(a) Randomized experimental designs (dealt with on page 44)

These are mainly efficient at eliminating threats to internal validity, i.e. the causal conclusions we infer from our data. Whatever approach is used it is vital to have some working criteria for assessing the quality of research into treatment programs. Gurman and Kniskern (1978) list criteria derived from reviews of the field of family and marital therapy. They suggest the following indicators:

- Controlled assignment of clients to treatment conditions: random assignment, matching of total groups or matching in pairs.

- Pre–post (i.e. before-and-after) measurement of change.

- No contamination of major independent variables: this includes therapists' level of experience, number of therapists per treatment condition and relevant therapeutic competence.

- Appropriate statistical analysis.

- Follow-up: three months or more.

- Treatments equally valued: tremendous biases are often engendered for both therapists and patients when this criterion is not met.

- Treatment carried out as prescribed or expected.

- Multiple change indices used.

- Multiple vantage points used in assessing outcome.

- Outcome not limited to change in the 'identified patient': this criterion is perhaps uniquely required in marital and family therapy.

- Data on other concurrent treatment.

- Equal treatment duration in comparative studies.

- Outcome assessment allows for both positive and negative change.

- Therapist–investigator non-equivalence: earliest reviews found the two to be the same person in about 75 per cent of the studies examined.

Studies of outcomes/achievment of objectives constitute a perspective or approach which is adaptable to many settings. What you do is:

- agree on *attainable* goals or objectives;

- agree on what will constitute evidence that a given objective
  has been achieved; i.e. what will be the criteria of 'success'
  of (for example) the acceptable standard of performance of a
  volunteer undertaking training in (say) assertive behaviour;
  or the level of improvement desired for a depressed patient
  receiving treatment in a drug trial;

- decide on some form of measurement;

- control for the 'placebo effect'. The reaction of a patient to
  the mere *fact* of receiving therapy can be so powerful that
  it is important to discriminate between the *fact* (referred to
  as the placebo effect) and the *act* of treatment in
  interpreting outcomes.

(b) Single-blind clinical trials

The purpose of using an inert substance (placebo) in a drug trial
is just that: a comparison of a series of inactive tablets with
pharmacologically active tablets (the X ingredient). This procedure, where the patient is 'blind' to whether he or she is
receiving the X ingredient, helps to mitigate an important con-
sumer source of bias. As such, this is a single-blind clinical trial.
But what of the investigator's expectations and attitudes?

(c) Double-blind clinical trials

A double-blind trial will mitigate (or preferably, eliminate) this
source of bias in the evaluation of medication. The researcher is
also made 'blind' as to which patient is receiving the inert placebo or the active drug. Bias can also creep in, in the selection
of patients for treatment and/or subjects for investigation; and it
is here that complete randomization is a preferred design (see
selection of research subjects, page 48).

Before-and-after research designs of the kind that figure in the
categories described above have been criticized when applied to
educational (behavioural objective type) research because they
assume that innovative programmes undergo little or no change
during the period of study. This is our cue to examine the issue
of qualitative data before looking at those research strategies that
make much (although not exclusive) use of such evidence.

CHAPTER 3

Quantitative versus Qualitative Methods

The research strategies described so far are mainly (certainly not exclusively) concerned with quantitative statistical procedures. But there are many research problems in the social services and mental health fields that lend themselves to more subtle, qualitative and language-based methods. This is a matter of particular significance to psychotherapists and counsellors who question the value of a 'hard-nosed' scientific approach to their work. Hardiker and Littlewood (1987) highlight this dilemma in their description of the distinction that is made in the research methods literature between *quantitative* and *qualitative* approaches.

They state that *quantitative research* rests upon certain positivist assumptions about the nature of social reality and the methods by which it can be 'known'. Positivists (they say) employ tight, preselected and prestructured conceptual frameworks, sampling frames, research questions, data collection instruments and methods, data reduction, coding and analytical techniques. These methods, when applied in an appropriate context — a good example is the evaluation of an innovative educational programme — impose artificial restrictions on the scope of the investigation.

Parlett and Hamilton (1978) maintain that a concentration on seeking quantitative information by objective means can lead to one missing or neglecting other data, perhaps more salient to the processes under investigation. Such information is downgraded as 'subjective', 'anecdotal' or 'impressionistic'. They make the point that research of this type, by employing large samples and seeking statistical generalizations, tends to be insensitive to 'local perturbations and unusual effects'. Atypical results are seldom studied in detail despite their possible significance. Such an evaluation often fails to come to grips with the varied concerns and questions of participants or protagonists in the programme.

There could be said to be a polarization of opinion about the role of empirical research methodology in psychology, such that Child (1973) speaks of two psychologies: the 'hard' and 'soft' (which tends to mean the 'humanistic') varieties. He expresses the contrast as follows:

> The soft psychologies are . . . faithful to and aware of the immediately felt reality of human experience and human personality. They take as their starting point the multi-diversity of the integrated person as he knows himself and is known to others. From this starting point it is not easy to move on to a scientific investigation; to framing limited questions testable by systematic observation. The soft psychologist may not see this as a great inadequacy. He wants first of all to be faithful to human reality as he knows it. He hopes a psychology that takes the conscious experience of the organized person as its subject matter will eventually lead to understanding man better than can a psychology that denies these obvious realities or clings to precise methods even at the possible expense of irrelevance.

In an attempt to define the essence of humanistic psychology Graham (1986) describes its aims as 'tranformation' promoting a qualitative change in being through the development of awareness.

She is sceptical about the place of scientific method in validating humanistic approaches. As she puts it:

> [Humanistic psychology] focuses on experience and feeling rather than fact; subjectivity rather than objectivity; and its concerns are precisely those excluded from scientific method. Therefore, to evaluate humanistic psychology in terms of the extent to which it meets the standards of science is invidious.

The proponents of qualitative research argue that in any event the 'hard' brands of objective evaluation tend to fall short (when the subject is complex) of their own desiderata of enforcing precise and unambiguous controls of extraneous influences. Innovations in practice are particularly vulnerable to the demands for control; the traditional evaluation is restricted by the dictates of its paradigm to produce generalized findings along *pre-ordained* lines. The scientific researcher's definition of empirical reality is, of necessity, constrained.

But social reality — according to the critics — cannot be

defined or understood in a manner detached from the person construing, studying or constructing it; measurement can destroy meaning and tear subtle processes out of the context that gives them meaning. Social realities are (in this view) too complex, relative and emergent to be measured with standardized instruments. A pharisaical insistence on inflexible and predetermined procedures — what some critics disdainfully allude to as 'scientism' or 'quantiphrenia' — leads to tunnel vision, binding the researcher to the letter rather than the spirit of scientific enquiry. He or she may well miss potentially important features of phenomena being analysed.* Serendipity goes out of the laboratory window.

According to Hardiker and Littlewood (1987), qualitative research tends to come into its own in 'natural settings' in relation to the very complicated, under-researched areas, where the paradigms require a phenomenological or inductive, interpretive ('in-depth') approach. The search for a new paradigm of research makes for an interesting and contentious debate. Sadly it is not possible to do justice to the issues here.

There is, in fact, some convergence between quantitative and qualitative methods, for example in content analyses (page 72). Which approach to adopt depends upon the purposes and objectives of the research and, for students, the constraints imposed by regulations on their endeavours. This begs the question — for this book — of the aims and concerns of clinical training and thus 'apprentice' clinical research. It is my contention that the scope of counselling (to take one example from the field of intervention in the helping professions) would require both quantitative and qualitative methods of enquiry. Parlett and Hamilton (1978) call for a total reappraisal of the rationale and techniques of programme evaluation. Their answer to the rigidities of experimental evaluation is described next.

Illuminative evaluation

The 'anthropological' research model (so-called) attempts the measurement of 'educational products' (one also thinks of 'therapeutic products') by means of intensive study of the programme

---

* Paradigms often predetermine procedures. A paradigm is a conceptual framework — a body of assumptions, beliefs and related methods and techniques shared by a large group of scientists/practitioners at the same time. Paradigms *are* useful in providing directions for research, permitting intensive and focused investigations. However, paradigms also determine what 'facts' are to be gathered and how they are to be interpreted (see Kessel, 1969; Kuhn, 1970). They can thus move from the positive enhancement of knowledge to the buttressing of intellectual obscurantism.

as a whole: its rationale and evolution, its operations, achievements and difficulties. The programme is not examined in isolation, but in its context.

Observation, interviews with participants ('consumers', teachers, therapists, administrators and others), questionnaires, analysis of documents, and background information are integrated to help 'illuminate' problems, issues and significant features of the programme.

The observation phase occupies a central place in illuminative evaluation. The researcher collects a continuous record of ongoing events, transactions and informal remarks. At the same time he or she seeks to organize this data at source, adding interpretations of both manifest and latent aspects of the situation. In addition to observing and documenting the day-to-day activities of the programme, the investigator may also be present at a wide variety of other events (e.g. seminars, meetings, case reviews) (see Parlett and Hamilton, 1978).

Much of the on-site observation involves recording discussions with and between participants. These provide additional information which might not otherwise be apparent or forthcoming from more formal interviews. The language conventions, slang, jargon and metaphors that characterize conversation within each milieu can reveal tacit assumptions, interpersonal relationships and differences in status. There is also a place for codified observation, using schedules for recording patterns of attendance, utilization of time and facilities, as well as interpersonal interactions.

To summarize the main feature of *illuminative evaluation* (see Miller, 1983; Parlett and Dearden, 1977), the methodology:

- is practitioner-orientated;

- is problem-centred;

- is flexible;

- is cross-disciplinary; and

- is heuristically organized, i.e. the research issues are progressively redefined as the study goes on and new data emerge.

This approach should be particularly applicable to the subtle and ever-changing nuances of humanistic counselling processes and their evaluation. It also lends itself to such programmes because of its serendipitous, flexible qualities. Unfortunately, it is impossible in an introductory guide to *do* justice to this form of evaluation, or draw out its precise applications to social casework, educational, psychotherapy or counselling research.

For those practitioners who valiantly try to evaluate their work as a matter of course, many of the available experimental designs must seem rather time-consuming, remote or irrelevant. The next approach is one which you may find directly applicable, or in some way, adaptable to your purposes.

Patient series research

It is clear, as we have seen, that experimental designs — be they of the large control/contrast group or small *N* type (see Hayes, 1981) — do not always fit the exigencies, idiosyncrasies and ethical imperatives of day-to-day practice. Patient series designs have their place in such circumstances. They involve painstaking investigation of individual patients coupled with a comprehensive analysis of the features of each case. The work of Masters and Johnson (1970), in many of its features, exemplifies this approach. It is an approach that finds a valuable methodology in the so-called case study.

The case study

This method is often the basis for psychological and clinical research. This is *not* necessarily a 'soft' or unrigorous option. Bromley (1986) claims that the individual case study or situation analysis is 'the bedrock of scientific investigation'. If this is really so, and the author provides evidence, we have not only an invaluable clinical method, but also a research tool. Bromley provides a general-purpose procedure for studying 'persons-in-situations' — something of interest to clinicians and counsellors — and thus a means of describing relevant facts and of organizing this information in a meaningful way. He demonstrates how a case study can be evaluated critically and in detail. His claims of the case study go well beyond their acknowledged role as illustrations or analogues of some wider category of theory or their application as creative-exploratory instruments.

The case study method, if applied rigorously, can, in his view, lead to genuine scientific discoveries and can establish genuine truths in their own right, i.e. it is capable of probing the plausibility and testing the generality of a theory. According to Bromley (1977), a case study involves a reconstruction and interpretation of a segment of an individual's life-story — based upon the most reliable evidence available. He refers to the process as the quasi-judicial method; it embodies a theory about how and why a person behaved as he or she did in a particular situation.

This theory should be tested:

- by collecting evidence; and

- by marshalling rational arguments to support the claims made in the theory.

The quasi-judicial method requires (inter alia) *that*:

- the main issues be stated clearly from the very beginning;
- sufficient empirical data be available to support or refute any claims;
- evidence be admissible and relevant to those claims;
- arguments be relevant and rational;
- conclusions which have important practical implications be backed up by a greater weight of evidence than conclusions of lesser significance.

Procedures

There are ten steps required by the explication of both individual cases and general laws:

- State clearly the problems and issues.
- Collect background information.
- Put forward *prima facie* explanations (conjectures/ hypotheses) and solutions (programme formulation) with regard to the client's personality and predicament — on the basis of information available at the time, and on the basis of the *principle of parsimony*. Examine the simple and obvious answers first. They may, of course, have to be rejected if they don't stand up to critical examination. This guides the search for further/additional evidence. New hypotheses/explanations will have to be formulated and examined.
- Search again for and admit for consideration sufficient evidence to eliminate as many of the suggested explanations (hypotheses) as possible, in the hope that one of them will be so close to reality as to account for all the evidence and be contradicted by none of it. The evidence may be direct or indirect; but it is vital that it should be admissible, relevant and obtained from competent and credible sources.
- Enquire critically into the *sources* of evidence, as well as the evidence itself. Bromley (1977) makes the point that in the case of personal testimony this is analogous to cross-examinations in a court of law; otherwise it amounts to checking the consistency and accuracy of all items of evidence.

- Examine carefully the internal logic, coherence and external validity of the entire network of hypotheses formulated to explain the clients' predicament and proposals to solve the problems.

- Select the 'most likely' interpretation, provided it is compatible with the evidence (some lines of argument will be obviously inadequate whereas others will be possible or even convincing).

- Work out the implications of your explanations for intervention/treatment or some other action (or indeed, inaction). Work it out in clear and specific terms, with stated and explicit objectives.

- Prepare the case report as a 'scientific account' of the client. It should contribute to psychological or social 'case-law' in virtue of the abstract and general *principles* employed in explaining the tactical adjustments or strategic adaptation of the person dealt with. Psychological case-law evolves out of systematic comparisons and contrasts between individual cases (Bromley, 1986). We are invited to discriminate between case and statistical inference since the case study is a 'strong form of hypothetical-deductive theorising, not a weak form of statistical inference'.

As Bromley notes:

> A well-argued case study is one which by its choice of materials and by its mode of reasoning, is robust enough to withstand critical appraisal as an explanation of a certain class of events . . . individual case studies derive their scientific merit not so much, if at all, from their representativeness or typicality, but rather from the insights they convey as vehicles for scientific explanation.

Bromley argues that since case studies can be used creatively or heuristically (in the context of proof/disproof) to test theories, there is a solid case for recognizing the value of this method in *basic science*, and not only in *practical* applications to specific clients.

CHAPTER 4

Assembling the Evidence

This is the crucial 'nuts and bolts' stage of your project where you finalize the practical and fine details of your research plan: sketching out the experimental design (if it involves an experiment), and selecting and assigning subjects to groups for testing on measures you have chosen.

Young (1966) describes a research design as the logical and systematic planning and directing of a piece of research:

> The design results from translating a general scientific model into varied research procedures. The design has to be geared to the available time, energy and money; to the availability of data; to the extent to which it is desirable or possible to impose upon persons and social organizations which might supply the data. . . . the most meaningful and revealing studies are those that are conceived from a definite point of view, but the views are modified as necessary in the process of study, as well as those that are dominated by a definite set of scientific interests which can be enlarged or curtailed, as the study in process requires.

For an invaluable review of fundamental design issues see Judd and Kenny (1981, pp. 223–229). It is my experience of supervising student research projects that many (especially the evaluative ones) would take at least five researchers five years to complete, if allowed to go ahead! So do be cautious and plan with care.

STEP 4: PLAN THE DETAILS OF YOUR STUDY

There are three essential questions to attend to:

- *What* is the nature of the research design required to answer my research questions (i.e. test my hypothesis)?

- *Who* am I studying (i.e. who do I select as subjects for my investigation and who goes into what groups)?

- *How* do I measure their performance on the variables in which I am interested? (This will be the subject of Chapter 5.)

THE 'WHAT?' QUESTION

The important issue here is the *precise* nature (which means specification) of the independent and dependent variables. The hypothesized relationship between these variables must be formulated clearly in terms of their operations. Thus: *The hypothesis predicts that that treatment (which involves operations A, B and C) will produce an effect (measured by tests X, Y and Z).* The null hypothesis, conversely, states that the treatment will not produce an effect. This, in essence, is what you test by means of your experiment/s. In the light of the data you obtain you reach a conclusion: either you *reject* the null hypothesis or you *fail to reject* the null hypothesis.

Let us now look at some of the finer details of experimental designs you have to choose from:

A simple experiment: two groups, one treatment condition

At the simplest level you can conduct an experiment to study two values of a single independent variable. You do this by administering a low level or placebo version of the treatment (independent) variable to *control group* subjects and a higher level of the independent variable to the *experimental group* subjects. At, or near the end of the experiment, you observe/measure how each subject performs on the dependent variable, an index of the subject's behaviour or performance.

The central concern in most research designs (including this simple one) is one of *control*. It is vital to relate the outcome of your study (say, a dependent variable such as an increment in self-help skills in handicapped clients) to the factors that are of particular concern to you (say, a specific training method). You have to control (i.e. exclude) the influence of extraneous factors. If you can achieve this you have what is called 'internal validity' (incidentally, you will also have achieved 'external validity' if you can generalize these findings (relationships) to similar clients in other settings).

To establish internal validity with a simple experiment use independent random assignment to create two samples that accurately represent your entire population of subjects. In this design each subject in a sample of (say) 16, has a different number; no subject bears any special relationship to any other. Say we are looking at a treatment condition *X* and a control condition *Y*. Our 16 subjects would be selected by using a random numbers table. Or else you could place their names in a hat and mix them thoroughly; the names would then be drawn out two at a time and the tossing of a coin would decide which of the pair was assigned to condition *X* (the other, of course, going to condition *Y*; see Table 1).

TABLE 1. INDEPENDENT SUBJECTS

Condition *X*		Condition *Y*	
S1	J.L.	S 9	A.G.H.
S2	S.P.McC.	S10	T.O'H.
S3	A.M.	S11	M.V.
S4	N.T.I.	S12	L.S.P.
S5	A.O'L.	S13	R.B.
S6	P.S.	S14	A.A.
S7	V.P.T.	S15	K.B.
S8	N.L.	S16	E.J.S.

The initials represent imaginary names of subjects (Ss).

The mean of the control group scores is an estimate of what would have happened if all the subjects had been in the control group. The experimental group mean is an estimate of what the mean would have been if all the subjects had been in the experimental group. The vital question is as follows: would all your subjects have scored differently had they all been in the experimental group than if they had all been in the control group?

Statistical significance tests (see page 77) are designed to answer this question. If the results are statistically significant, the difference between your groups is greater than would be expected by chance (random sampling error) alone. Therefore, you reject the null hypothesis and conclude that *your treatment has an effect.*

Blocked design

Ideally this design should give you more power (see page 49) than a simple 'between subjects' design of the type described above. Your experimental subjects are subdivided into groups (blocks) on a subject variable that you are concerned with (e.g. a severe level of handicap block and a moderate level of handicap block). You now randomly assign subjects from each block to the experimental condition.

Maxwell (1958) states that in a well-planned experiment the need for adopting a proper system of *randomization*, which ensures that chance is given full scope, is essential. He deprecates the tendency for 'amateur statisticians' to take statistical tests and formulae from books on statistics and present them cut and dried and, as it were, ready for general use. When developing the theory the mathematician will probably have made certain assumptions — perhaps that 'errors' are purely random and may be assumed to be normally distributed, or that the 'samples' which he or she has in mind are unbiased, etc. These assumptions are made to simplify the mathematics and so enable the mathematician to present results in a concise and usable form.

The experimenter, when employing the theory, must plan his or her experiment in such a manner that these assumptions in the theory are met. Maxwell goes on to say that:

> . . . the design or structure of an experiment — and here the process of randomisation is included — is, in the words of catechism, 'the outward and visible sign' of the assumptions made in the mathematical theory. To apply a statistical test to data without regard to the manner in which the data are obtained is like putting the ingredients for a cake into the oven to bake, ignoring completely the instructions to stir them until they are thoroughly mixed. And as the stirring must be done before baking takes place, if it is to be done at all, randomisation must be performed before the data are collected and analysed, otherwise the opportunity is irretrievably lost.

Multiple groups: more than one treatment condition

You can expand a simple experiment by making use of several independent variables (i.e. multiple treatment conditions). Obviously, if several treatments and/or levels of treatment and several groups are required to test hypotheses, the research design becomes a good deal more complex. The name *factorial experiments* is given to designs that examine two or more independent variables (factors) at any one time.

Randomized experiments *are* the design of choice if you wish to maximize internal validity, i.e. reach *causal* conclusions about treatment effects. Ideally, the researcher selects subjects at random; assigns subjects to groups at random; and assigns experimental treatments to groups at random. Unfortunately, the large numbers involved in such a design, as applied to the evaluation of therapies, usually limits its implementation to a research team with substantial resources.

A good example of the use of randomization is to be found in the treatment trials carried out in medical/psychiatric settings. The researchers decide on the criterion or criteria for selecting patients and allocate them on a random basis to treatment and placebo conditions. There is no pairing or grouping of patients on the basis of particular patient characteristics for the purpose of obtaining some balance in the distribution of patient characteristics between the different treatment groups. The assumption is that the patients can more or less be considered relatively homogeneous with respect to the outcome variables.

It is, in part, the relatively large number of patient characteristics itself (e.g. age, sex, level of formal education, class) in relation to the comparatively small number of patients in any one investigation that makes grouping or pairing prior to the allocation of treatment an inevitably incomplete and usually unrewarding procedure. There are so many potentially confounding variables to control that one doesn't know where to begin.

There are distinct advantages in the use of a multi-condition (i.e. multiple-group) experiment. If, for example, medical researchers were comparing four different therapies plus a 'waiting list' (temporary 'no-treatment' condition) on a series of outcome measures, they could conduct a series of simple experiments. But think of the number of experiments they would have to perform: ten in order to compare all five conditions one with the other. Then there is the sheer number of subjects to investigate. To have a reasonable degree of power (see page 49) they would need 15 subjects per group. That means for 10 simple experiments (20 groups) a total of 300 (20 × 15) subjects. With one multi-value experiment they would obtain the same power with 75 (5 × 15) subjects.

To analyse data from a multi-group experiment, researchers commonly use analysis of variance (see page 89).

The 2 × 2 factorial design

This design allows you to study two independent variables (say assertion training and relaxation training) in a single experiment.

You would randomly assign subjects to four groups: (a) a no-assertion-training, no-relaxation training group; (b) a *no*-assertion-training, relaxation-training group; (c) a *no*-relaxation-training, assertion-training group; and (d) a relaxation-training, asssertion-training group. You would measure the effects of these group combinations on (for example) outcome measures indicating increased self-confidence in social relationships. There are as many as eight basic patterns of results you could obtain from the main effects of the two independent variables and their interactions in a 2 × 2 experiment.

Your independent variables may combine to produce an unexpected effect — a so-called *interaction*. Interactions are nicely *illustrated* in graphical representations of your data (see Figure 8; see also Mitchell and Jolley, 1988, for a valuable guide to the analysis of factoral design data).

Expanded 2 × 2 design

It is possible to expand the 2 × 2 design by adding more levels to one or both variables. Thus, if you were studying the effects of homework and a home token economy on exam performance, you could use three levels of homework (1, 2 or 3 hours of study) and three levels of incentive (say three levels of monetary reward). Factorial designs can be elaborated as much as you like, but there are likely to be diminishing returns when the data become too complex to interpret.

The matched-pairs experimental design

You might wish to compare a new reading teaching method with the traditional reading method. The matched-pairs design would help you to resolve the issue of which is most effective. In this research design you first measure your subjects on a variable that is related to the dependent measure (say, pre-test reading comprehension scores). Now you form *matched pairs* of subjects who have similar scores on the reading comprehension tests.

The 16 subjects in the design illustrated in Table 2 are numbered in pairs. The members of a pair have been *matched* on the salient variable (in this case reading comprehension scores). The two subjects with the highest scores are assigned to number 1; the next highest to number 2, and eventually the lowest to number 8. A coin is now tossed in order to determine for each pair which member goes to condition X (new reading method), and which to condition Y (traditional reading method).

As you can see from Table 2, this design combines the virtues of matching *and* randomization. Matching reduces

TABLE 2. MATCHED SUBJECTS

Condition X		Condition Y	
S1x	V.B.	S1y	G.E.
S2x	S.W.	S2y	P.B.O.
S3x	A.T.D.	S3y	R.B.
S4x	R.G.	S4y	J.B.
S5x	D.H.	S5y	R.H.
S6x	K.C.T.	S6y	D.W.
S7x	V.D.	S7y	L.P.M.
S8x	J.F.C.	S8y	T.D.Y.

extraneous confounding factors and randomization helps to establish internal validity (see page 31).

Given certain attributes (see page 88) intrinsic to your data and your measures (e.g. scaling), you can analyse your results by means of the *dependent groups t-test* so as to compare the two reading methods — condition X and condition Y (statistical methods are discussed in Chapter 7).

Within-subjects research design

This design is useful where test results are likely to be biased by factors such as practice effects, fatigue and other lingering 'carry-over' influences. What you do is to obtain two scores from a single subject rather than (as was the case in the preceding design) from a pair of subjects. The researcher uses randomization to determine for each *individual* the order in which he or she will get each treatment. For some the first treatment will be condition X, while for others it will be condition Y. The dependent groups t test can be applied to your results.

Counterbalanced research design

You may wish to study two levels of a factor (say two variations of a physiotherapy exercise for a physical disability). In this design you randomly assign half your subjects to receive routine X first and routine Y second. The other half would receive routine Y first and routine X second. If subjects do better on the second trial this will not advantage routine X more than routine Y as both have occupied the second position equally.

With more treatment conditions, counterbalancing obviously becomes more complicated as we see in the example in Table 3, in what is called a *Latin square*.

TABLE 3. THE 4 × 4 SQUARE (treatment conditions W, X, Y, Z)

Order	1	2	3	4
Experimental group 1	W	X	Z	Y
Experimental group 2	X	Y	W	Z
Experimental group 3	Y	Z	X	W
Experimental group 4	Z	W	Y	X

You can see that treatment W occurs in all four order positions, as do treatments X, Y and Z. There are variations and combinations of Latin squares to help you achieve balance when you have more (and uneven) numbers of condition.

The pretest–posttest research design

This is similar to the AB design (see page 24). Instead of comparing one person's performance before and after treatment, you include several subjects in your pretesting, administer the treatment or training and then test them again at the termination of the programme (see Herbert, 1987a).

Time-series design

This quasi-experimental design involves making a *series of observations* from a group of subjects over time, before and after they receive the treatment. Trend analysis will help you to determine the nature of any relationship between the independent variable and dependent variable.

There are other research designs which are outside the scope of this guide. A few to be aware of, because of their value in estimating the effects of clinical, social and educational interventions, and also maturational influences, are the following (see Judd and Kenny, 1981; Mitchell and Jolley, 1988):

- The regression discontinuity research design.
- The non-equivalent control group research design.
- The interrupted time-series research design.
- The changing treatment research design.
- The post-only correlational design.
- The cross-sectional research design.
- The longitudinal research design.

THE 'WHO?' QUESTION

Your selection of subjects for the research project will be influenced by your research design, the scope of the task you've set yourself and plain expediency — the availability of subjects.

If the population you wish to study is relatively small (say all the children with cystic fibrosis in one hospital, or even in a local group of hospitals) you could decide to test or survey all of them. If not, you sample the population that you are interested in. There are special procedures for obtaining any sample you use (e.g. random, quota or stratified). Each has a particular rationale (see Som, 1973):

Random sampling

In random sampling (as we've seen) each member of the population has an *equal probability* of being selected and the selection process must be *independent*. This means that the selection of a particular subject must have no influence on the selection or exclusion of other members of the population from the sample. There are ways of doing this properly (see page 44 for an example of a completely randomized clinical trial).

Quota sampling

This is designed to ensure that your sample matches the population on certain characteristics, e.g. male : female, social class membership, age, ethnic membership. Unlike the next method, quota sampling does not involve random sampling.

Stratified random sampling

You ensure by this method that your sample is similar in make-up to the population in important particulars. If you were studying adolescent conduct disorders (say), you know the population is roughly 3 :1 boys : girls in rates of incidence. So you make sure your sample is 66.3 per cent male and 33.6 per cent female. You divide your population (stratum) into two subgroups (substrata): male and female. You decide on how many individuals to sample from each substratum (say 66 boys, 33 girls). Next you draw *random* samples from each substratum. (Where you had one sample from the main population in random sampling you've collected two samples from two substrata.) Of course you might wish for many more than two substrata, as would be necessary in a Gallup poll.

Sample size

The size of your sample is decided in the light of both theoretical *and* practical considerations. My advice is 'take advice'. The generalization (if any) that you can make about your findings depends on the nature of your research sample, so your decisions in this area cannot afford to be frivolous. A rule of thumb (very rough) for beginning researchers is to use as large a sample as is feasible, given the constraints of time, availability of subjects, and other relevant circumstances operating in your research setting.

Whenever an average (mean), a percentage or some other statistic is calculated on the basis of a sample (say, one in ten of the schizophrenic patients in the UK) a *population value* is being estimated (i.e. the figure for *all* of the schizophrenic patients in the UK). How much error is there likely to be in the statistics calculated from samples of different sizes? To put it simply, the smaller the sample the larger the error! There are tables which provide more precise, quantified answers to this question.

Power

The 'power' or sensitivity of an experimental design refers to its ability to actually find an effect if the sought-after effect is a reality. Generally speaking, power can be enhanced by either increasing the number of subjects or by increasing the amount of data (say, number of observations) recorded for each subject in $N = 1$ or small N research designs (see Cohen, 1977).

When it comes to thinking about the *content* (as opposed to the *size* of your sample) remember that there are advantages *and* disadvantages in having tightly defined, homogeneous groups of clients. Certainly the use of clearly, indeed narrowly, specified categories of subjects reduces the 'within-group' variance (see page 89), thus increasing the power of the experiment. In addition, other researchers will be able to replicate your work when there are clearly identifiable subjects to seek out.

The major disadvantage arises from the generalization issue:

are your results with X patients typical of patients with similar problems 'out there' in the wider world? Also, as Berger (1980) points out, there seems to be a law that says: 'when you have identified a particular group of subjects who would be just right for your study, every specimen disappears off the face of the earth'. So be prepared to have difficulties locating subjects with particular characteristics, especially if their characteristics are somewhat unusual, for instance, extroverted, exam-phobic 18- to 20-year-old female students with no medical signs of ill-health, whose parents have intact marriages and a middle-class background. The more precisely you specify your target group the less easy it becomes to find them.

To summarize: the kind and quantity of subjects you actually need will be determined by factors such as the characteristics of the group you wish to study, the numbers required in your subgroups if you are required to subdivide them, and ultimately the number needed to satisfy the assumptions of your design and data analysis; and as I said before (and it is a particular problem in the case of student projects) a key factor is the sheer availability of subjects.

In the case of students/trainees you *must* work out the time you have available. It is possible, and *may* be acceptable, to do an intensive study on one subject or a study with 100 subjects. How many you need is dictated by what you are able to manage (you could give questionnaires but not in-depth interviews to 100 subjects) and how much you want to be able to say, and generalize about, when the conclusions are stated. Your particular research question requires an individual, rather than a formula answer, when it comes to sample constituency and size.

By the end of this stage your research design should be finalized. This will be your blueprint for action — the point where your ideas are translated into *actions*: the collection of data. This is our cue to look at the methods (techniques, tests and instruments) for collecting evidence in the form of readings, scores, verbal reports, signs, symptoms, counts and many other indices of performance of one sort or another.

CHAPTER 5

Generating Your Data

THE 'HOW?' QUESTION

How are you going to obtain your data? It is essential to select methods and instruments with great care so that they will be consistent with the points on reliability and validity raised later in the chapter. You may wish to use structured, semi- or unstructured interviews, focused interview schedules, observation schedules, questionnaires or coding books. But do not go on a 'fishing expedition' — a battery of anything and everything you can think of — in the hope of finding something interesting. Such mindless trawls usually bring in mindless results.

Some of the methods and measures described below lend themselves to the collection of *nomethetic* (interpersonal/normative/standardized/group comparison) data; others are at home in the intra-individual approach — the intensive quantitative and/or qualitative analysis of psychological processes in the client. This is the so-called *idiographic* approach (see Allport, 1937).

Some of the most rigorous testing methods produce the most trivial answers if their choice is predicated on exquisitely precise, but essentially banal, questions. This is *not* to make a virtue of being unrigorous and certainly not to deter you from quantitative work where it is feasible. Qualitative analyses — which go some way to capturing the subtleties of therapeutic processes — demand of their users the same respect for evidence as other approaches.

Reliability and validity

The outward and visible signs of good measurement are reliability and validity. *Reliability* refers to the stability, dependability and predictability of the tests/methods you are using, in other words their *precision* or *accuracy*. If your measurements are reliable then you can be confident that they are relatively immune from random error: temporary, chance fluctions. Would two testers using the same measuring instruments obtain similar results? Would a tester obtain a similar result using the measuring instrument on different occasions? These are questions about reliability.

Every test has an error component, that is to say the person's 'observed score' is made up of a hypothesized 'true score' (the true measure of, say, the person's intelligence or IQ) plus an error score. Any one test gives only an estimate of the person's true score. There are several ways of checking the reliability of testing instruments (see Anastasi, 1982):

- *Test–retest*: you administer the same test after an interval of time to the subjects of the reliability investigation.

- *Split-half*: you split the test items into two matched halves and then correlate the obtained scores.

- *Alternate forms*: you give equivalent versions of the same items to your subjects and the obtained scores are then correlated.

Unless you are constructing your own test you should be able to find a good measuring instrument for your specific purpose — good, if it publishes empirical (and satisfactory) indices of the test's reliability and validity. If you do have to carry out your own test construction, consult a psychometric textbook *and* (preferably) an expert. Test construction is a complex and very time-consuming matter (Mitchell and Jolley, 1988).

You can find out from the manuals of well-constructed and carefully standardized tests just how much *error of measurement* is associated with their use (e.g. Anastasi, 1982). To be interpretable, a test *must* not only be reliable but also valid.

Validity refers to whether a test measures what it purports to measure. A test is unlikely to be valid if it is not reliable, although a test can be reliable without being valid. The issue of validity is a complex and contentious issue. There are several forms of validity:

- *Content validity*: this refers to the representativeness/ sampling adequacy of the content of the test.

- *Criterion-related validity*: this is the validity estimated by comparing the test outcome with one or more external variables, or criteria, known or assumed to measure the attribute under consideration.

- *Decision aspects*: this form of validity depends on whether the test is able to solve problems and make decisions. For example, some would say that IQ tests predict academic performance, at least in a restricted sense, and therefore aid the making of decisions. Others, of course, have contested this claim for the validity of IQ tests in the school setting.

- *Construct validity*: this refers to the validity of the *theory* that lies behind the test. Here the interest is in explanations — confirmed ones — of the test and what it is measuring.

Source material

Methods are reviewed in Buros (1978), Bellack and Hersen (1984), and other source books or specialist journals. These publications provide the detail you require for selecting tests and other instruments. Remember that many tests are of dubious validity, so it is advisable to take advice or look up the test literature.

Let us now take a look at some of the investigative methods at your disposal:

The interview

Interviews provide chiefly three kinds of information:

- observations of a limited sample of behaviour manifested during the interview;

- data about the client's present situation and predicament;

- life-history data.

What the person has done in the past is a good indicator of what he or she may do in the future, especially when interpreted in the light of *concomitant circumstances* and of his or her comments regarding these actions. The interview is used to find out not only what happened to the client, but *also* his or her perception of those events — the meaning ascribed to them and the current evaluation put upon them.

Miller (1983) provides the guidelines illustrated in Table 4.

Unstructured interview schedules are usually relevant to exploratory research. Sometimes a combination of structured data-collection instruments and unstructured, open-ended methods will be employed.

Questionnaires

Questionnaires are likely to be used in many research projects, sometimes as adjuncts to interviews. Many people decide to

TABLE 4. METHOD: INTERVIEWING

Range of types	Advantages	Disadvantages/ biases	Safeguards
Structured (standardized, pre-specified questions. The same words used to each interviewee with questions given in the same order)	Enables responses from different individuals to be compared	Does not allow interviewee to explore an issue in his own terms Questions may not be relevant to interviewee	Careful 'pilot study' of questions
Semi-structured (a 'core' of standard questions or topics, with other questions generated from the interviewee's responses)	All individuals' responses can be compared on the 'core' questions, while other issues spontaneously raised by the interviewee can be taken account of	Interviewer could bias responses in deciding which answers to follow up	Tape record interviews and use outsiders to judge interpretations Joint interviews making separate notes and cross-checking later (but note that they may both have the same biases). Let the interviewee check a transcript of the interview
Open-ended (interviewer raises the issue to be discussed, and interviewee talks about it in his own way)	The interviewer's own concepts do not predetermine the interviewee's account, and he is able to express his own views freely A skilled interviewer can obtain very sensitive and personal data	Difficult to analyse such 'rich' and variable material Difficult' to validate one-off interviews Requires considerable skills both in obtaining information and interpreting it	Use outside judges Compare findings with other types of data Use 'devil's advocate' to put forward other possible interpretations

TABLE 5. METHOD: QUESTIONNAIRES

Range of types	Advantages	Disadvantages/ biases	Safeguards
Close-ended (range of possible answers specified with the question) *Semi-open-ended* (prespecified answers, with encouragement for open comments; or some questions open-ended)	Can be given to large numbers of people simultaneously and who may be widely distributed geographically Standardized wording and order of questions means responses can be compared	Respondent may not be able to reply because the questions do not use the concepts, the constructs or the vocabulary that mean something to him May be filled in under widely different (non-standard) conditions	Preliminary study to determine relevance of questions and vocabulary
	Anonymity for respondents	May be low percentage returned	
	Can be filled in respondent's own time Relatively speedy way of collecting data	No way of checking whether respondent has understood questions in way intended Biasing responses by choice of questions and range of prespecified answers	'Back-translation' — ask sample people to go through their own questionnaire explaining their answers
Open-ended (each question represents a topic and the respondent is asked to comment freely on it)	Respondent can answer from his own point of view, selecting what is relevant to him	Mass of data difficult to analyse Difficult to compare with other respondents	
		Researcher bias most likely at data analysis stage Respondents may be put off by open format which provides few cues to the answers	Analysis done independently by several different individuals who then develop a common framework

make up their own questionnaire as it seems a fairly simple and very convenient thing to do. Sadly it is far from simple; in fact it is a veritable minefield for the unwary — one in which booby traps such as response bias, wording difficulties and item selection are waiting to 'blow up' your proud creation. Having been a Job's comforter let me now encourage you to design your own questionnaire *if* there isn't a ready-made one of repute available. But *do* take advice!

Table 5 gives guidelines for the use of questionnaires as research instruments, provided by Miller (1983).

Observation

One of the most direct ways of measuring behaviour is by observation of interpersonal interactions. Fortunately, there has been considerable research into the measurement of behaviour by direct observation (see Browne, 1986; Martin and Bateson, 1987). Observations are made prior to the research intervention and they can be repeated at different times during the programme. A painstakingly detailed interview about the client's typical day can produce reliable and valid data supplemented by direct observations, also records and diaries (Herbert, 1987a).

It is wise to make observations according to some predetermined schedule. This is an important precaution against the bias that would arise if the observer merely recorded whenever something obvious or interesting happened. The time at which the recording session starts and stops should be determined in advance unless, of course, the aim of the study is to discover what occurs during or after a particular type of behaviour has occurred.

Miller's (1983) guidelines are given in Table 6.

Observational data

There are several methods for analysing observation-based research (see Browne, 1986).

Frequency analysis

(a) *Proportional frequency* scores are necessary to take account of varying lengths of observation sample time. To compare every parent (in a study of parental behaviour), each behaviour item can be calculated as a proportion of the total number of time interval units per episode, e.g. 'scolding offspring' might total 18 units of a total of 36 observed units, and would receive a score of 0.50 for that sample.

TABLE 6. METHOD: OBSERVATION

Range of types	Advantages	Disasdvantages/ biases	Safeguards
Unstructured (records as much as possible using no pre-arranged format)	Observations responsive to a wide range of activities	Observer may suffer overload trying to take in too much at once	Observations may become successively more focused. Have several observers recording different things
Semi-structured (observing events according to a prespecified schedule, and measuring rates at which they occur)	Able to make on-the-spot record of events, not relying on someone else's recall. (Applies also to structured observation)	He may see only what he wants or expects to see	Have more than one observer take notes independently and cross-check
	Can observe those who cannot talk (applies also to a structured observation)	The presence of the observer may produce atypical behaviour	Have 'dummy runs' while people get accustomed to observer
Structured (observing events according to a prespecified schedule, and measuring rates at which they occur)	Enables different settings to be compared on the same observational criteria. Relative ease of analysing the schedules once the coding has been done	The items on the schedule may not fit what is happening in the setting	Draw up the schedule for use in a particular context having observed more flexibly first
		The observer may ignore otherwise significant events in order to keep to the schedule	Have two observers — one keeping to the schedule, the other more open
		The schedule may not specify the kinds of behaviour which constitute an 'event' to be categorized	Training in the use of the schedule (perhaps with aid of video) to exemplify different categories

Range of types	Advantages	Disasdvantages/ biases	Safeguards
		May miss 'crucial' events	
Active participation (observer joins in all activities of those he is observing)	Observer becomes accepted as one of the group, not an outsider	His own actions may radically alter what the group would have done	Go along with the group rather than initiate action
		May 'go native' — lose objectivity, take actions for granted	Report frequently to an 'outsider' colleague who questions assumptions. Frequently review early field notes
Passive participation (no part in activities; or presence unknown to group)	Does not disrupt normal activities of group and is free to observe	Passive presence may make group feel uncomfortable. Ethical problem sometimes in being unknown	Note how group treats observer over time. Talk to members about the effects of a passive outsider

(b) *Interaction frequencies*: for every parent and offspring the total number of time units spent on interaction can also be calculated as a proportion of the total number of observed time units in the sample. The number of (say) initiating and responsive interactive behaviours could then be determined and calculated as a proportion of the interaction score for the observation time.

Types of interaction may be identified in the following manner. The parent is eating and the offspring reaches for the food (interactive initiative); the parent may give the offspring some food (mutual interaction), stop eating and attend to the offspring (causal interaction), or continue to eat (failed interaction).

Bout analysis

The duration of an 'interaction bout' can be established by summing the number of time-interval units that occur in sequence, containing an ongoing interactive behaviour between parent (say) and offspring. The start and finish of such a sequence can be determined by periods of non-interactive behaviour.

Sequential analysis

Recent studies of human relationships can be distinguished by the emphasis on temporal relationships and contingencies of behaviour, in interactive situations. Dyadic interactions are based on the interweaving of the participants' behavioural flow as time passes, and sequential analysis is a powerful method for analysing this behavioural flow.

The simplest type of sequencing of events is a 'deterministic sequence' where events always follow each other in a fixed order, so that the nature of the preceding act defines precisely the nature of that which will follow. But most behavioural sequences are 'probabilistic' rather than 'deterministic' in form, meaning that while the probability of a given act depends on the sequence of those preceding it, it is not possible to predict at a particular point exactly which behaviour will follow. If the sequences are highly ordered they are usually referred to as 'chained responses'. In these cases, the probability of a particular event is markedly altered by the event immediately before it. If the sequences are not so highly ordered, some transitions may be observed between almost every behaviour and every other, and only those transitions which have a high probability of occurrence are then useful.

In the parent–offspring case, sequential analysis can be applied initially by determining sequences within the individual, for example, if a parent shows act *A* it could be interpreted as an indication that activity *B* may follow if the parent shows *B* after *A* more frequently than any other behaviour. However, the sequences within the parent may also depend on what the infant does, and activity *B* might follow *A*, only if the infant shows activity *C*. Therefore, the determination of interindividual sequences is important.

Thus sequential analysis can yield three types of data:

1. Sequential flow of behaviour for parent.
2. Sequential flow of behaviour for infant.
3. Sequential flow in interactive behaviour between parent and child.

There are many ways of monitoring behaviour — from the molar to the molecular — some of which (and the sheer amount of time given to them) are more suitable to laboratory-clinical research than to the work of a hard-pressed trainee or busy practitioner. The following list gives an idea of the range of measures available:

Time budgets

A record is made of the time the person devotes to his or her various daily pursuits. Such a record kept over many days is likely to betray significant interests and reinforcers as well as personal idiosyncrasies (distractibility, procrastination, preoccupation and the like).

Time sampling

This procedure involves direct observation of the person's behaviour; the attention of observer and analyst is fixed upon selected aspects of the stream of behaviour as they occur within uniform and short time intervals. The duration, spacing and number of intervals are intended to obtain representative time samples of whatever is being investigated. Such 'field observations' may involve records of children at home, in nursery schools, boys and girls in camp, patients in hospital, students at their studies, and so on. In other words, they represent a sampling of natural, everyday situations.

Event sampling

This method begins with a plan to study events of a given kind, e.g. outbursts of temper tantrums in children or cooperative acts by adolescents doing some common task in the work situation. The investigator stations himself or herself where the people involved can be seen and heard, waits for the events to happen and then describes them in great detail.

Trait rating

The observer, after several sessions of observation, uses a rating scale to sum up what he or she has seen of the client's traits, e.g. friendliness, low self-esteem, anxiety, jealousy and so on, having defined them first in operational terms, i.e. in terms of observable behaviour.

Sociometry

This so-called 'nominating technique' is a procedure in which each member of the group is asked to name the members of the group with whom he or she would like to work, play or engage in other designated activities. Naming may not always be the method used. An observer may simply plot the interactions of a group to see who is isolated, popular, gregarious, etc.

Situational tests

These tests place the client in a situation closely resembling or simulating a 'real-life' situation. A long-stay patient — rehabilitated and returning to the community — is an applicant for a position. He or she is asked to play a role as an interviewee confronted by a potential employer.

Rating scales

There are several types of rating scale (five or seven-point scales seem to be most popular).

(a) *Numerical rating scales*: The rater assigns to each ratee a numerical value for each attribute. The numerical values may be defined in semantic terms. For example: a rating on serious-mindedness of 7 might mean 'takes everything as if it were a matter of life or death'; of 4, 'neither serious nor unconcerned'; of 2, 'ordinarily unconcerned and carefree'; of 1, 'seems not to have a care in the world'; etc. Such ratings would best be anchored in agreed and clearly observable behaviour.

On a Likert-type scale, subjects usually respond to a statement by ticking off either 'strongly agree' (which gets a score of 5); 'agree' (4); 'undecided' (3); 'disagree' (2); or 'strongly disagree' (1). The Likert scale is assumed to yield interval data (see page 81).

(b) *Graphic rating scale*: This is a variant of the numerical scale. The judgement is made by marking a point on a line to define the client's position between two extremes:

How anxious is the subject?

			X	
Extremely	Very	Some	Mildly	Not at all

Personal construct tests

There are a number of techniques available (e.g. the Q-sort technique, the Semantic Differential and the Repertory Grid) which allow for the direct expression of the personal conceptual system — the manner in which the individual 'construes' or conceptualizes himself or herself, other people and the world they live in. They may reveal constructs, and relationships between constructs, that the person is barely aware of, or which function normally at an implicit rather than verbally explicit level. For example, an individual may be construing her husband in much

the same way as her father, and thus negatively, and a test like
the Repertory Grid helps to point out such connections (Bannister and Fransella, 1980).

Behavioural measures

High-speed cameras, microcomputers, tape recorders, video-
tapes, stop-watches, etc. are used to record, measure, collate
and time large segments or sequences of behaviour (molar
behaviour). For example, computerized event recorders record
observations directly on to a keyboard and store them in a digital
form, suitable for analysis by a computer. Observations can now-
adays be recorded directly on to the keyboard of a portable,
unobtrusive microcomputer (see Bakeman and Gottman, 1986;
Browne, 1986).

Physiological measures

Electroencephalograms are used to measure electrical activity in
the brain. A galvanic skin response apparatus is used to measure
the electrical resistance of the skin. Various apparatus measure
blood pressure, heart rate, muscular tension, and so on. There
are instruments to record several physiological measures simultaneously.

Written activity records

Diary description, the oldest method used in the study of child
development, employs the client's (or therapist's) diary to draw
up an account of the sequences and changes in the client's
behaviours and interactions. The use of an activity or job diary,
for example, is among the most simple and popular ways of
finding out how a person's time is spent; the use of a child-
management diary provides valuable data on the interactions
(and confrontations) between parents and their children (Herbert, 1987a, b).

The critical incident technique provides a way of identifying
the 'noteworthy' aspects of a person's life — his or her behaviour
at work, or in social situations, etc. Critical and non-critical tasks
are defined and recorded (see Flanagan, 1954).

Portfolio approaches record information about how a problem
has arisen, and the methods used to solve it.

Related to these methods is the use of written autobiographies
or self-characterization with older children and adults. They may
reveal all shades of attitude to self, other people, activities, and
so on.

The intensive methods rarely make use of control subjects,

although the individual may act as his or her own control. This implies measures of *change* and requires an understanding of designs that incorporate reliable measurements of change, be they phenomenological (e.g. self-report), behavioural (e.g. a series of target behaviour ratings) or physiological (e.g. penile plethysmograph measures) over time. Of course, many of these measures can be used within both the nomothetic *and* idiographic modalities.

Measurement is fraught with theoretical and technical difficulties. Matters such as a systematic response bias, reactivity to observation, errors of measurement, reliability and validity are discussed in texts on psychometrics (e.g. Anastasi, 1982). Be alert to their implications! Unfamiliarity with the snares and traps of psychological measurement could make nonsense of your findings, negating the time and energy you've given to your research project.

PART II
Initiating Your Project

Remember that there are usually complicated *practical* details to work out before you actually begin testing. There are logistical problems to sort out with regard to the arrangement and timing of testing sessions or interviews. (Use a calendar to draw up a detailed and dated flowchart of testing sessions.) There may be ethical committees from whom you have to obtain formal approval, and so on. Do not leave these administrative arrangements until the last minute. For complicated, many-sided research programmes, there are 'network' systems which help you to order your research activities (see Howard and Sharp, 1983).

You will need to decide whether your questionnaires (for example) will be completed by respondents or yourself, and how you will record the data arising from your interviews, e.g. by taking notes (verbatim or condensed) or on tape-recorder. It is advisable to pre-code the questionnaire. If you are scoring tests plan the response sheets or test booklets with great care. The layout of subjects' response-sheets can be planned for easy scoring, perhaps by means of a stencil key. By consulting computing staff you may be able to plan a layout that is immediately applicable to key punching for computer analysis.

List the people (clients, agency staff, administrators, students, public) who will be asked to provide the actual data for your questions, or be involved in obtaining permissions or making arrangements. Check *who* does *what* to *whom, when*.

THE PILOT STUDY

If you are a novice in any of the areas you are going to research — indeed, even if you are not — run a 'dress rehearsal', i.e. a pilot study. By the end of this pilot investigation (keep it as short as is necessary to test out your methods, time them, ensure that instructions are comprehensible, etc.) you should be able to administer your research methods smoothly and accurately. You have the opportunity to iron out difficulties and unforeseen complications. There usually are some. What may cause a radical change in the shape of the study, or (more usually) a simple improvement in method (say, a reduction in test items) or an acceptance of more modest goals, is the experience gained from the trial run.

CHAPTER 6

Collecting and Analysing Your Data

It is important to give each person in the study a unique identifying code and to record the date and time the data were gathered.

STEP 5: COLLECT THE DATA

Once you begin the study (collecting data) keep detailed notes on its progress. These notes will consist of impressions of the reactions of the subjects, the workings of the instruments and any other observations which might be relevant to your study. Occasionally in data analysis you encounter data from one subject which are unusual when contrasted with the results from the rest of your group ('outliers'). It is legitimate, given proper justification, to discard such findings. If you have kept notes at the time you were gathering the data you may find you have good reasons for rejecting them.

Debriefing — a discussion of the subjects' experience of the research process — is becoming a feature of evaluative research; such discussions may provide valuable insights into your study. They can help in the interpretation of results. Talking to subjects about their experiences lets them know that you regard them as people and not as mere 'subjects'.

STEP 6: ARRANGE, ANALYSE AND INTERPRET THE DATA

It is useful to think of the data analysis as a process of exploration. Johnson and Pennypacker (1980) manage to inject an erotic metaphor into the calm world of data analysis by noting that 'as in amorous foreplay, the process of exploring one's data should proceed from the general to the particular, aided at every step by enhanced visualization'. More mundanely you need, on the one hand, a map — a conceptual/theoretical framework — constructed from what you already know about your subject. This allows you to make informed choices and decisions. On the other hand premature foreclosure — reaching facile conclusions or making erroneous assumptions too early — will stop you from seeing things in the data that you didn't expect to see.

Quantitative analysis

Essentially you wish the data to speak for itself. This requires a step-by-step process (see Hartwig and Dearing, 1980).

(a) *Set out* the data in a manner that allows you to look at it clearly and think about it (e.g. displaying it by plotting scores in histograms, frequency polygons, setting out scatter diagrams (Figure 4), or, tabulating frequency data in different ways (e.g. high Xs; low Xs versus high Ys; low Ys). Graph your data where relevant. In the case of a histogram and frequency polygon, start by labelling the x-axis (the horizontal axis) with (say) units indicating the frequency of particular scores and labelling the

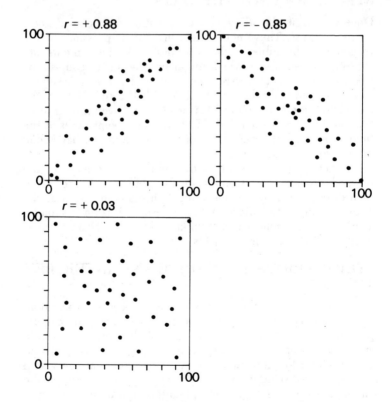

Figure 4. Scatter diagrams illustrating the association between two variables represented by various correlations

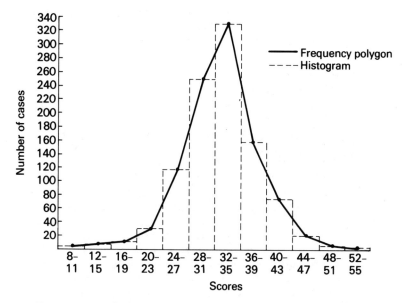

Figure 5. Distribution curves: frequency polygon and histogram

y-axis (the vertical axis) with the measured/tested variable. Then plot each observation (see Figure 5).

(b) Where there is a large data set you will need to *summarize* it without distorting it. Means, standard deviations, correlation coefficients and regression models are typical examples (see page 76) of the statistical approach to summarizing data.

Kerlinger (1986) defines statistics thus:

> Statistics is the theory and method of analysing
> quantitative data obtained from samples of observations
> in order to study and compare sources of variance of
> phenomena, to help make decisions, to accept or reject
> hypothesised relations between the phenomena, and to aid
> in making reliable inferences from empirical
> observations.

If you are measuring change you will have to display the data so as to highlight its stability, trends, changes in means and variability. In the case of single-case research there is some debate about whether to use statistical and/or visual inference — matters too technical for a book of this scope (however, see Kazdin, 1982, for a full discussion of the issues).

(c) Do not treat the data in a static, one-dimensional manner; look at it from different angles, trying out — in your search for meaning — different patterns/combinations of your data. Relationships you might have thought to be linear (Figure 6a) may be non-linear (Figure 6b).

(d) Inevitably your analysis involves the selection and editing of data. Just as there are several varieties of research design there are different ways of analysing data. The approach you adopt depends on the questions you want answering, i.e. *your particular research problem*, not some predetermined, prescriptive and (therefore) arbitrary specification of the 'correct' way of doing things. Remember, there *are* horses for courses!

Whether the data are produced numerically, statistically or in the form of rich illustrations from interview transcripts, you must follow certain rules and provide safeguards against 'manufacturing' your data. As Hardiker and Littlewood (1987) put it:

> Some case illustrations may be more interesting than others, but you should endeavour to select examples from a representative sample of responses; furthermore, some of the hunches you have about your data may not be confirmed by your evidence . . . it is important to spell out the methods you have adopted, and the difficulties you may have encountered and possibly overcome during your research.

A valuable text on exploratory data analysis is that of Tukey (1977). It is very tempting to get side-tracked into irrelevant analyses, especially now that computers can very quickly perform all sorts of clever tricks. You should avoid this temptation; computers are no substitute for thoughtful analysis. The balance is between imaginative but thoughtful 'play' with your data and mindless 'number crunching'. As the cynics so elegantly put it: 'Garbage in, garbage out!'

The task is to impose order on the multiplicity of facts, verbal responses or numbers you have generated. In the case of numbers, study your raw data closely before you do any statistical analyses; their distribution will tell you if the data are distributed normally or (at least) have a form acceptable for the type of analysis intended.

Qualitative analysis

Your data — if derived from a qualitative study — may be untidy with no clear boundaries — a mass of verbal responses which somehow eludes your grasp at first. This is to be expected if your data reflect experiences drawn from 'real life', as is likely to be the case in (say) psychotherapy or counselling research.

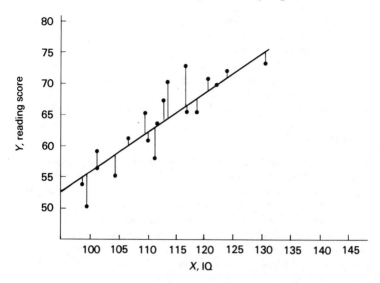

Figure 6(a). Scatter diagram illustrating a linear relationship between IQ and reading score (the points are linked to a straight line — see page 84 — this is called the linear regression of Y on X)

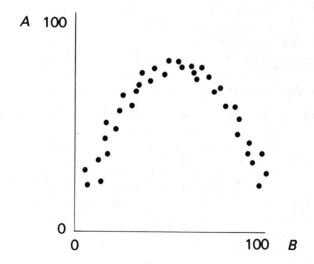

Figure 6(b). Scatter diagram, showing an inverse U-shaped relation between two variables (A and B). The association between A and B is strong, but non-linear. However, the Pearson correlation between them is zero ($r = 0.0$)

You are also likely to have collected more data than you can write up in your report.

Where you have a good deal of qualitative data (e.g. verbal responses to an interview) ask yourself several questions — queries that move from the descriptive to the analytical, and on to the synthetic. One example of this progression, referred to as a content analysis, based on Miller (1983), is provided below.

Content analysis

This is an invaluable tool for use (*inter alia*) in psychotherapy and counselling research as it provides a method of categorizing a wide range of open-ended (unrestricted) responses, for example, analysing *communications* in a systematic, objective and quantitative manner. The availability and flexibility of computers (see Appendix B in Kerlinger, 1986) make the application of content analysis to verbal material (e.g. that produced in response to projective techniques or therapeutic sessions) much simpler than used to be the case. The major units of analysis are words, themes, characters, items and space-and-time measures. You take the communication that people have produced and ask searching questions of these communications (see Holsti, 1969).

Here are some key questions drawn from the illuminative orientation — which combines elements of both qualitative and quantitative analysis — described by Carolyn Miller.

What has been covered?

Make a simple list of all the *topic areas* covered by the data.

What have I found?

Collect the data together under each of these topic headings, e.g. for interviews, extract what each person said about the topic. A brief note and a reference to an interview page number can save time.

This gives you in one place all the opinions (or observations) about a particular topic. You can now check how many people shared an opinion. For example, your impression that, say, quite a lot of counsellors favoured time-limited as opposed to 'open-ended' counselling programmes may now be seen to be nine out of 20 people. Many topics will not be open to such precise counting, but you will be able to see the weight and variety of opinion when you see the quotations next to each other. Miller reminds the researcher of Sherlock Holmes' curious case of the dog that didn't bark when it might have been assumed that it would. Are there any topics notable for their absence from the list — a topic which you thought was going to be important but which was hardly mentioned?

How does it hang together?

Here Miller is referring to the relationship of one topic to another: take the topics on your list and look for relationships between them, then discard the idea of a linear list, and draw up a pattern to show the points at which topics link with others. The 'branching tree' structure or diagrams with linking arrows may prove helpful. These enable you to begin clustering information, to make connections between one kind of happening or opinion and another.

What does it all mean?

Are one or more general *themes* emerging from the clusters of information? Such themes and types can be used to structure the writing of the report. But if there are no obvious recurrent themes then they should not be forced; the clusters of topics will suggest the headings for the different sections.

It is not possible to begin to do justice to the intricacies of content analysis in a broad-based text such as this one; however, do consult the technical references (methods) and, in particular, Holsti (1969).

Data analysis as problem solving

Brooks and Watts (undated) in their comments on research dissertations make the point that researchers all too often think in terms of simple statistical recipes (is that a *t*-test problem?) rather than in terms of using their data *to solve problems*. They go on to say of some trainees:

> When asked in the oral examination to state in commonsense terms how they had approached their data analysis ('Were you looking for differences in frequencies; for associations; for differences in central tendency, etc., etc?') many researchers simply cannot say what the goals of their data analysis were. They tend to refer instead to the statistical test that they had used, and defend the use of tests by simple devices such as saying 'My supervisor told me to do it'. It is as important to know *why* particular analyses were done as to carry out analyses appropriate to the data. In addition to this very major conceptual problem, they often seem unaware of basic statistical concepts.

This is our cue to look at the role of statistics in our quest to understand our data, to solve research problems and thus to arrive at reasonable conclusions. Ferguson (1966) has this to say:

> Implicit in any experiment is the presumption that it is possible to argue validly from the particular to the general and that new knowledge can be obtained by the process of inductive inference. The statistician does not assume that such arguments can be made with certainty. On the contrary, he assumes that some degree of uncertainty must attach to all such arguments, that some of the inferences drawn from the data of experiments are wrong. He further assumes that the uncertainty itself is amenable to precise and rigorous treatment, that it is possible to make rigorous statements about the uncertainty which attaches to any particular inference. This is the uncertain milieu of experimentation he applies to a rigorous method.

If you are not familiar or confident with the 'language' of statisticians, the following chapter (which is *not* about formulae) introduces some terms and concepts — and, in particular, applications — which may be helpful to you.

CHAPTER 7

Statistical Analysis

Statistics are a means to an end — a useful end of making good sense of your data and describing them economically. Sadly there is an 'off-putting' mystique about the subject such that what should be a researcher's 'good friend' is approached by many as an enemy. Indeed the approach may have been put off until it is too late, i.e. when the results are already to hand.

Maxwell (1958) is concerned that the student may get a misleading picture of the function and scope of modern 'statistical science'. He or she may — as a beginner — conclude that:

> Statistics deals mainly with the calculation of means and medians, the purpose of which may well be clear enough; standard deviations and standard errors, the value of which is seldom immediately obvious; or, correlation coefficients and other measures of association which, incidentally, are inherently dangerous in all but experienced hands. At the higher reaches he may conclude that statistical methods are synonymous with tests of significance themselves. The latter conclusion, in particular, would be unfortunate, for though these tests form an integral part of statistical procedure they represent only one aspect of it — equally important are the estimation of 'error' itself, or of the magnitude of a 'real' difference — and are themselves validated by the neglect of other aspects. To be more explicit, the emphasis in statistical methodology has, in quite recent years, passed from the *analysis* of data and the isolated use of tests of significance, to the *design* of experiments.

Statistics can be classified in terms of the various functions they serve:

Multivariate analysis

On page 43 we looked at the statistical assumptions that might go hand in hand with *randomized experimental designs*. A very important tool in the analysis of the many and varied (and complexly interacting) variables that play a part in the psychology of persons is called multivariate analysis. This is a general term covering a group of analytical methods whose chief attribute is the simultaneous analysis of k independent variables and m dependent variables. They enable the researcher to tease out the influence of each variable from a whole set when some or all of them have been affecting the project. Suppose, for example, you wish to know the likely duration of a stay in hospital for illness X. Age, sex, severity of illness and medication level (dosage) are all relevant. How is one to predict length of stay from these various factors? The technique called *multiple regression* achieves this by correlating, i.e. measuring the degree of association between all possible pairs of variables (age and medication level, age and severity, severity and medication level, etc.) and analysing all the relationships so as to produce an equation indicating the best predictors. Other statistical techniques — best studied in specialist statistical texts — include factor analysis, canonical correlation, discriminant function and analysis, log linear analysis, path analysis and analysis of covariance structures (see Harris, 1985; Kerlinger, 1986).

Do not despair if some of this is 'double Dutch' to you. Statisticians are employed (*inter alia*) to give advice to those of us who are not highly numerate or confident with the more sophisticated statistical methods. This is not an excuse to avoid familiarizing yourself with foundational statistical theory and methodology (Hays, 1981; Howell, 1982), and the questions that the more complex statistical techniques have been designed to answer (see page 84).

Descriptive statistics

These statistics help us to describe data by reducing large quantities of numbers to a manageable and understandable (in other words, *summary*) form. They include measures of *central tendency* (means, medians and modes); measure of *dispersion, scatter* or *variability* (variances, standard deviations, ranges); and measures of *association* (correlation coefficients).

When we are told the mean of a sample, even though we have not seen the distribution of (say) scores, we can surmise certain things about it — that the scores distribute themselves both above and below the mean value, and that in some sense they are balanced around it.

Sampling statistics

These statistics tell us how well the statistics we obtain from measurements of single samples probably represent the larger populations from which the samples were drawn (a matter discussed earlier).

All statistics have 'standard errors'. A standard error is an index number that leads us to conclusions concerning how far the statistic derived from the sample probably differs from the value we would obtain if we had measured an entire population. These statistics help you to make reliable inferences from observational data. For example, it is possible to 'conclude' that methods X and Y *really* (i.e. reliably) differ. Or it is possible to conclude from evidence of a correlation coefficient (a measure of association of a particular size) that two variables are *really* related.

Decision-making statistics

If we need to decide which of several (say) methods of counselling best facilitate marital harmony in a difficult marital situation, or which organization of service delivery most benefits an 'at risk' group (with the least 'cost'), there are statistics to help you obtain the information you need (Cronbach and Gleser, 1965).

Tests of significance

Knowing how much groups of subjects differ in their results in some medical or psychological investigation doesn't tell the researcher how much of an effect the treatment (independent variable) had. A sceptic might say that the entire difference between groups could have resulted from *random sampling error*. This is where tests of significance come into their own: to determine the probability that the difference is not due exclusively to extraneous (chance) factors. If, by applying statistical tests, you establish that the difference between your groups is larger than could be expected if only chance were operating, then your findings are *statistically significant*. This means that you are certain, beyond reasonable doubt, that this outcome would be repeated in a *replication* (repeat experiment) because it is not a fluke.

There is a caveat to all of this! If you carry out a large number of tests of significance in your experimental analyses — say 100 — and use a 0.05 level of significance (see page 79), five of those tests could be significant by chance alone.

At the simplest level, tests of significance are concerned with the straightforward comparison of sample means. For example, a geriatrician may wish to compare a sample of elderly clients with Alzheimer's disease (group 1) and a sample of similarly aged clients with a depressive illness (group 2) in terms of their performance on a battery of 'cognitive-function' tests. He or she is interested in developing a useful screening device. The question which must be faced when the data has been collected is as follows: 'How great must the difference be between the mean scores of group 1 and group 2 to allow me to think of them as forming *separate* populations (as regards their performance on cognitive tests) instead of one *homogeneous* group?' In other words, do cognitive tests reliably differentiate elderly patients with one form of dementia from elderly patients suffering from clinical depression?

Let us now express the statistical task in a more elaborate way with a different example. Suppose that you have been testing out a parent training programme for a number of months in the home setting, as well as one in a child psychiatric out-patient clinic of the general hospital. The same tests were used in each setting and you have gradually accumulated a sizeable file of test results. You notice that the results from the home setting seem to be different from those obtained at the hospital clinic and you begin to consider whether these represent real (i.e. reliable) differences.

The logic of testing for significance is quite simple (see Hays, 1981): the statistician's answer to the problem of significance of differences is expressed in terms of probability:

- The null hypothesis (H_0) that the means do *not* differ is formulated.

- The next step is to calculate a summary measure (a measure of central tendency) for the test scores from each, e.g. a mean.

- If the null hypothesis is true then you would expect the means to be similar, and the difference between them to be 'small'. How small 'small' actually is can only be assessed from a reference distribution which shows what the distribution of differences would be if the null hypothesis should happen to be true.

- By using an appropriate reference distribution, you can calculate the probability that a difference at least as large as the one observed would occur by chance if the null hypothesis were true.

- If the probability is relatively large, so that the obtained difference might be expected to occur by chance (say *more than* once in 20 times), then you fail to reject the null hypothesis.

- If the chance probability of obtaining a difference of the magnitude you have actually found is sufficiently small — less than one in 20 ($p < 0.05$) or (if you are being very cautious) one in 100 ($p < 0.01$) — then the null hypothesis is rejected, and the result is taken as indicating that the population means are indeed (significantly) different. This leads to the statement: 'The difference in responses (as measured by various tests) to home-based therapy and hospital-based therapy is statistically significant at the 5 per cent level ($p < 0.05$).' Unfortunately you can go wrong when you account for chance influences. There are two types of errors which may be made in arriving at a decision about the null hypothesis.

- Despite there being no difference between the means one might obtain an extreme deviation as a consequence of sampling error. This could well be the case in the example above. This results in the *rejection* of the null hypothesis even though it is true (i.e. saying there is a statistically significant difference when there isn't one.) An error of this type — mistaking a chance difference for a treatment effect — is called an error of the first kind, or a Type I error (also, in diagnosis as a 'false positive', for example, a patient diagnosed as sick when he or she is in fact well).

- On the other hand, we may get the case where there *is* a significant difference between means; the samples *are* from separate populations. By chance we might get values which lead us to *accept* the null hypothesis, when in fact it is false (i.e. it should be rejected). This possibility of overlooking a genuine treatment difference because you think it might be due to chance is called an error of the second kind, or a Type II error (also, in diagnosis called 'false negative' — the patient is diagnosed as 'well' when he or she is, in fact, 'sick').

You can see — and it is a matter of great importance to medical researchers, in particular, because the risk is not academic — that you have to make a trade-off between the risk you are prepared to take of a Type I as opposed to a Type II error. You don't want to be reckless, nor overly conservative, so that you miss the real differences. You therefore want your investigation to have *power*, the ability to avoid making Type II errors.

Power

Mitchell and Jolley (1988) make the point that many undergraduate research projects are doomed from the start because they lack power. And, doubtless, this prognosis applies to many research programmes other than undergraduate ones. To increase the power of your research you reduce the effects of random error, and increase the size of your treatment effect.

To achieve these desiderata:

- Use reliable measures (see page 51).

- Use a homogeneous group of subjects.

- Code your data precisely.

- Use more subjects.

- Give your experimental and control groups very different amounts of the treatment.

Statistical tests are also said to have power (see Cohen, 1977). A statistical test is a powerful one if it has a high probability of rejecting the null hypothesis when it is, in fact, false, i.e. you will find statistically significant differences when they do actually exist. I return to this issue on page 83 when we turn to a brief discussion of parametric and non-parametric tests.

Negative results (floor and ceiling effects)

It is possible to find that two groups of subjects do not differ on (say) a vocabulary test, when in reality they do. This could be because all the scores are clustered at one or other end of the possible range of values. Differences will be obscured if all or most subjects obtain the minimum possible score (a *floor effect*) or the maximum possible score (a *ceiling effect*). For example, a test of ability involving the comprehension of simple words is unlikely to reveal differences between adults because most people will answer all the questions correctly (a ceiling effect). Clearly, a more difficult test is more likely to reveal differences, but a test that was too hard would result in most people answering none of the questions correctly (a floor effect). Although this point may seem obvious, it is often overlooked as a possible explanation when negative results are obtained.

Directional effects (one-tailed and two-tailed tests)

If your study (say a medical investigation of the psychological after-effects of local as opposed to general anaesthesia) involves a prior prediction — that the mean score for local anaesthetic patients on a battery of cognitive tests is higher than the general anaesthetic group — the test of significance you consult in the relevant statistical table could be one-tailed. There *must* be a genuine and *rational* prediction made before the results are generated.

If no direction is specified in advance (merely a statement that 'the scores will be different') you use the two-tailed test. In most cases a two-tailed test should be used. Many learned journals insist on the more stringent test (see Appendix IV). The point here — when you are looking up the critical values for a test statistic (such as a correlation coefficient or Student's *t*) — is that the critical value of the 0.05 level for a two-tailed test corresponds to the 0.025 level for a one-tailed test.

Scales of measurement

Something to be aware of is the limitation in the arithmetical and statistical operations you can perform with the numbers or scores you have derived from your chosen measures. You may be assigning numbers to categories (e.g. 0 = 'no improvement'; 3 = 'satisfactory improvement', etc.). In essence you are using a 'scale' of measurement.

It is common to distinguish four levels of measurement. From lower to higher levels of precision and sophistication we have: *nominal*; *ordinal*; *interval* and *ratio* measurement scales.

- *Nominal data* are the most basic, measuring differences in kind rather than degree. A number can stand for a word. Thus you might ask the question: 'How would you describe yourself as a parent?' and categorize the responses into 1 = strict; 2 = permissive; 3 = over-protective; 4 = *laissez-faire*; etc. The numbers merely denote differences — qualitative, not quantitative, differences.

- *Ordinal data* indicate that bigger means more, so 3 is more than 1 (which you cannot claim with nominal data). You cannot, however, assume that the difference between 1 and 3 is the same as that between 3 and 5. You have only ordered your data.

- *Interval data*, on the other hand, does allow you to answer not only the question 'is 3 more than 1?' but also '*how much* is 3 more than 1?' The psychological distance between 1 and 3 is the same as that between 3 and 5. Getting interval scale measurement is a complicated business (Anastasi, 1982) and is sometimes claimed when it is very doubtful that it pertains (e.g. on certain rating scales).

- *Ratio scale data* have an absolute zero and equal intervals —
  a perfect one-to-one correspondence between the numbers
  your test produces and psychological reality. If IQ measures
  were ratio measures (which they certainly are not), you
  could say that a person with an IQ of 100 was twice as
  intelligent as a person with an IQ of 50. It is difficult to
  think of a psychological measure that generates ratio scale
  numbers.

Constraints associated with levels of measurement

Different research questions require different levels of measurement:

- Are the subjects in group A more likely to be of the (say)
  extrovert *type* than the subjects in group B? (Nominal data
  are the minimum requirement.)

- Is group A *more* extroverted than group B? (Ordinal data
  are the minimum requirement.)

- Is the difference between group A and group B *as much as*
  the difference between group C and D? (Interval data
  apply.)

The scales above are also listed in the order of greater flexibility
of mathematical treatment. The higher the level of scale the
more we can do with the numbers we obtain in measurement.
You would not summarize nominal or ordinal data by calculating
means (averages). Percentages would be most appropriate (see
Table 7). This table is called a crosstab, as it allows you to
compare groups for similarities and differences.

TABLE 7. INCIDENCE OF VARIOUS TYPES OF
TEMPERAMENT

	Index group	Contrast group 1	Contrast group 2
Easy	4 (24%)	9 (53%)	15 (88%)
Difficult	5 (29%)	0 (0%)	1 (6%)
Slow-to-warm-up	5 (29%)	2 (12%)	0 (0%)
Intermediate	3 (18%)	6 (35%)	1 (6%)

To quantify the relationship between variables you would calculate a correlation coefficient. For nominal data it would be a *phi
coefficient* which, like other correlation coefficients, ranges from

+1 (perfect positive correlation) through 0 (zero correlation) to −1 (perfect negative correlation). With interval data you calculate *means* to indicate central tendency and correlation coefficients to provide measures of relationship/association (see references for further detail: e.g. Siegel, 1956; Schiffman *et al.*, 1981).

Constraints on statistical testing

Statistical tests cannot be applied indiscriminately. There are constraints on when and how you apply the more powerful *parametric* statistical tests. There are less restrictive non-parametric statistics available (see Siegel, 1956; Marascuillo and McSweeney, 1977) for studies in which the scaling is of a lower level or the distribution of scores is not normal. It is vital to be familiar with these constraints, not waiting until you come to your analysis, but before you design your study.

Parametric statistical tests

There are certain key assumptions that underlie the use of these tests, which include the powerful Student's *t*-test; analysis of variance; linear regression; and the Pearson correlation coefficient:

- Normal distribution: the data/scores follow a normal distribution (see Figure 7).

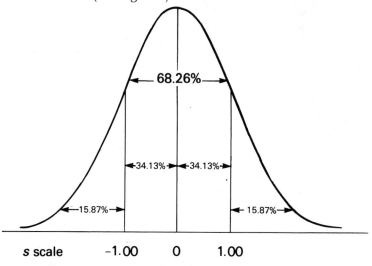

Figure 7. The Normal Curve, indicating the proportion of (say) scores falling below different areas (defined by standard deviation) of the curve

- Samples or subgroups have approximately equal variances *homogeneity of variance).*
- Associations between *variables* are *linear* (see Figure 6a).
- The effects of different conditions or treatments are *additive.*

Non-parametric statistical tests

The assumptions of such tests as the chi-square (χ^2), Spearman rank correlation, Mann–Whitney U test and Wilcoxon matched-pairs test are somewhat less stringent than the parametric tests. They are called *robust* because they are not dependent on such assumptions as normality of distribution or interval/ratio scaling. They can be used to analyse *ordinal* data. Indeed χ^2 can be applied to nominal data.

The main assumptions of these invaluable statistical tests (given the 'untidy' nature of behavioural data) are that measurements have to be independent, and (usually) variables have to display an underlying continuity, such as would be assumed in a personality dimension like extroversion–introversion.

The power of these tests is not always that much less than the parametric methods (see Martin and Bateson, 1987). In any event, although they may not be as powerful as parametric statistics and may thus fail to detect an effect that in reality exists, they are *conservative* in the sense that they are unlikely to produce a spuriously positive result.

Choice of statistical analysis

I have expressed this choice (in the manner of Siegel, 1956) in terms of answers — a list of appropriate tests — to specific statistical questions. Some of the tests are referenced only, while others are described briefly.

Question 1: Are two sets of scores associated?

To answer this question you have the choice of several coefficients. A correlation coefficient refers to the extent to which two measures (or variables) are related, that is to say, co-vary. A correlation of 1.0 represents a perfect association; every score on one measure is perfectly predicted by the scores on the other measure. This can be a positive prediction — a positive correlation (+1.0) or a negative one (–1.0), indicating a perfect inverse relationship. A correlation of 0 means that one set of scores tells you nothing about the other set. The following rule of thumb will help you to interpret, in semantic (informal) terms, statistically significant correlation coefficients of different magnitudes:

A Pearson r value of

- <0.2 represents a minute, almost negligible relationship.

- 0.2–0.4 represents a low correlation, definite but small relationship.

- 0.4–0.7 represents a moderate correlation, substantial relationship.

- 0.7–0.9 represents a high correlation, strong relationship.

- 0.9–1.0 represents a very high, very reliable relationship.

To compare Pearson correlations, use the square of the correlation coefficient (r^2). This figure (known as the coefficient of determination) is the proportion, broadly speaking, of the variation in one measure that is accounted for statistically by the variation in the other measure. A correlation of 0.9 means that 81 per cent of the variation in one set of scores is accounted for statistically by the variation in the other ($r^2 = 0.81$).

A correlation of 0.6 indicates that one measure accounts for 36 per cent of the variation in the other measure ($r^2 = 0.36$). A correlation of 0.9 is thus over two times as great as a correlation of 0.6, contrary to first appearances.

It is important to remember that correlational methods do not establish *causality*. You do not know whether the relationship between two variables is due to:

- changes in the first variable causing the second variable to vary;

- changes in the second variable causing the first variable to vary; or

- a third variable causing both variables to vary.

Here is a guide to the applications to which different correlation coefficients are put:

- *Pearson r* applies where both variables are measured in terms of interval data (say height with weight).

- *Point biserial* applies where one variable is interval, the other nominal (height with nationality).

- *Biserial* applies where one variable is interval and the other is a dichotomized interval variable (weight with high versus low scorers on a test).

- *Tetrachoric* applies where both variables are dichotomized interval variables (tall versus short with heavy versus light).

- *Spearman*'s *r* applies where data are ordinal-ranked data (classroom exam rank with sports achievement rank).

- *Phi coefficient* applies where both variables are nominal (gender with nationality).

Question 2: Is there a significant difference between the scores of two unrelated samples?

To take an example, is there a significant difference between the scores of two different groups of subjects? (Tests of difference between two unmatched samples.)

- *Chi-square* test for two independent samples (nominal data).

- *Fisher* exact probability test (nominal data).

- *Mann–Whitney U* test.

- *Student's t-test* for unmatched samples (this is a parametric test).

The Chi-Square (χ^2) test for two independent samples

This test is appropriate when you have nominal data: *frequencies* (counts) in discrete categories. The χ^2 test determines the significance of the differences between the two independent groups; that is to say, it tests the hypothesis that the groups differ in respect of some characteristic which is reflected in the frequency with which the group scores fall into the different categories. A geriatrician might have two conditions (reminiscence therapy versus no therapy) to which 50 elderly hospital residents have been assigned. The residents are categorized at the end of three months as 'improved' or 'not improved' on a sociability measure. The 2 × 2 table might look like this:

	Improved	Not improved
Reminiscence therapy	15	10
No therapy	3	22

The proportion of scores from each group falling into the various categories is compared, and the null hypothesis of no difference in these proportions is tested by a formula. Applying the test would tell if there was any relationship between reminiscence therapy and improved sociability.

The chi-square test for 2 × 2 contingency tables is widely used in research. Virtually all textbooks in statistical methods recommend that the chi-square test (Pearson's chi-square) should not be employed for 2 × 2 contingency tables if the expected frequency in any cell falls below five. With small cell frequencies, the probability derived from the chi-square test is thought to be an unsatisfactory approximation to the true probability, because large-sample theory is used in the derivation of chi-square. See Camilli and Hopkins (1978) for a different view of this issue.

The Fisher exact probability test

This is applied where these conditions cannot be met (see Siegel, 1956).

The Mann–Whitney test

This is a test of significant differences for two independent samples where the data are ordinal and can be ranked. It is the non-parametric equivalent of the *t*-test below; it puts the two groups of scores together and rank orders all of them. Then it checks whether one group has mostly low ranks while the other has mainly high ranks.

The *t*-test for unmatched samples/groups

The *t*-test is applied to problems involving the significance of the difference between the means of two sets of scores obtained from independent samples. The test would come into use if your experimental design had investigated differences brought about in groups of independent subjects exposed to two experimental conditions/treatments. The differences are measured on one dependent variable. Interval or ratio data are necessary for this test. Scores must be normally distributed.

The basic aim is to compare the amount of variability due to predicted differences in scores between the two groups as against the total variability in subjects' scores. The predicted differences are calculated as a difference between the mean scores for the two groups, and the actual value of this difference is compared against the overall range and variability in scores. Total variance in scores is measured by a formula which takes into account the variability in individual scores around the mean. The statistic *t* represents the size of the difference between the means for the two groups, taking total variance into account.

Question 3: Is there a significant difference between the scores of two related samples/groups?

An example would be the difference *between the scores of the same subjects* under two different experimental or treatment conditions. These tests are thus tests of difference between two matched samples.

- Wilcoxon *Matched-pairs signed ranks test.*

- *Student's t-test* for matched samples ('matched-pairs *t*-test').

The Wilcoxon test

This is a non-parametric signed-ranks test for correlated samples, i.e. where you have matched-pairs data.

The Student's *t*-test for matched samples/groups

This correlated *t*-test is used when you have interval or ratio data obtained in experimental designs which test differences between two experimental/treatment conditions applied to one dependent variable. Thus you might be studying the effect of stress conditions (as compared with non-stress conditions) on autonomic nervous system (ANS) responses. The data are composed of pairs of measurements of ANS responding. These may be correlated; and this circumstance leads to a test of significance between means different from that for *independent* samples. The *t*-test formula takes into account the correlation between the paired measurements.

Question 4: Are there significant differences between the scores of several unrelated samples?

Here you wish to test differences between *k* unmatched samples.

- Chi-square for *k* unmatched samples.

- Analysis of variance.

Chi-square test for *k* independent samples (nominal data)

If the rating of improvement in the example given for the 2×2 contingency test (page 86) were a bit more refined: 'emotional improvement'; 'cognitive improvement'; 'social improvement'; and 'no improvement'; (a four-category scale), then you would apply $2 \times k$ (where *k* in this case equals 4) χ^2 contingency statistics.

Analysis of variance (Parametric/ANOVA and Non-parametric/Kruskall–Wallis)

One-way ANOVA — a parametric test — is useful if an experiment has one independent variable and more than two levels of an independent variable. It is used to test the significance of the differences between three or more means; in this sense it is a multiple *t*-test. As a parametric test it will require interval or ratio data. In an unrelated design any differences in scores between treatment conditions are also differences *between* groups of subjects. However, any differences between subjects *within* each group in each condition are due to irrelevant variables — referred to as random error.

Once the between-group variance (an estimate of the combined effects of random error and treatment) has been calculated, as well as the within-group variance (the estimate of random error in the data), you are on your way to finding out the influence (if any) of your treatment conditions. The *F* ratio tests the experimental hypothesis that the variance between conditions will be relatively large compared to the error variance of subject groups within each condition. If the treatment has no effect, the between-groups variance should be roughly equal to the within-group variance.

Because one determines whether a treatment had an effect by comparing (analysing) the between-group variance with the within-group variance, this statistical technique is called analysis of variance (ANOVA). Analysis of variance can be elaborated into more complex forms, such as the two-way analysis of variance (see Hays, 1981).

Interactions

Factorial experiments (as we saw on page 44) allow you to look at more than one variable or factor at a time, and the commonly used ANOVA provides a means of analysing the significance of effects of combining different levels of particular independent variables. When independent variables combine to produce an unexpected effect you have what is called an *interaction*. Interactions can most easily be observed by graphing your data; if the two lines are not parallel (as in Figure 8b and c) you have an interaction. If it is a statistically significant interaction you cannot discuss your *main effects* without referring to the interaction.

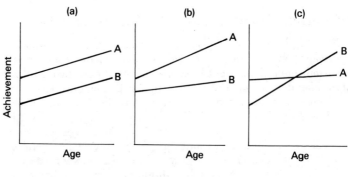

Figure 8.

The Kruskal–Wallis One-Way Analysis of Variance

This test is the non-parametric equivalent of the one-way ANOVA, also comparing different subjects performing under three or more different conditions. It tests whether the scores for the groups of subjects are significantly different. Differences between conditions are examined by ranking all the scores in a single series, and summing the ranks in each condition. The value of the differences between these rank totals is given by the statistic H.

Question 5: Are there significant differences between the scores of several related samples?

To take an example, are there significant differences between the scores of the same subjects measured under several different conditions? (Tests of difference between k matched samples.)

- *Friedman* two-way analysis of variance.
- *Repeated-measures analysis of variance* (this is a parametric test).

Question 6: Does the sample come from a specified population?

(Tests of goodness of fit for single samples.)

- *Chi-square* test for one sample.
- *Binomial test* (nominal data).
- *Kolmogorov–Smirnov* one-sample test.

Question 7: Are several sets of scores associated?

Are the scores of one group of subjects consistent when measured several times, or is there an overall association between several different measures for the same set of subjects? (Test of concordance between *k* rankings of the same subjects.)

- *Kendall coefficient of concordance*: a typical application of this test would be the assessment of agreement between people rating social skills based upon their observations of the same subjects behaving in identical experimental situations.

Here are a few more methods that you may find useful.

Principal component analysis and factor analysis

These statistical methods help you to tease out which variables are correlated with each other and distinct from other variables. A large number of variables can be reduced and expressed in terms of a smaller number of factors.

Multiple regression analysis

This method (touched on earlier) allows you to identify the combination of independent variables which predicts the dependent variable. The relative contributions of the independent variables to prediction can be estimated.

Discriminant function analysis

This is an analysis of the variables which best discriminate two or more groups of people from each other. It answers the question of how well these different groups can be separated.

Log-linear analysis

Here the analysis identifies which combination of independent variables predicts the dependent variables (usually dichotomous measures rather than the continuous measures more commonly found in multiple regression analysis).

Effect size

There is an important point to make before leaving the subject of statistics; it concerns the distinction to draw between the magnitude of an *effect* (e.g. the extent of the difference between the scores obtained by two groups) and its *statistical significance*. Effect size and statistical significance are not the same thing; the level of statistical significance does not correspond directly to the clinical significance or scientific importance of the finding. An observed effect could be very small yet highly significant in statistical terms, provided the sample is a large one. For the clinician the effects may be too small to be useful for diagnostic purposes.

Making use of microcomputers

Norris *et al.* (1985) make the point that statistical testing is not limited to elaborate research projects but can be applied to the important issues that arise in everyday clinical practice. Results, scores and readings are the 'bread and butter' of medicine; but they are often evaluated subjectively by the clinician. They add that this is understandable because statistical procedures

> . . . are time-consuming, and they do demand knowledge and expertise. It is an area ideally suited to a microcomputer which can easily store data and can perform arithmetic very fast indeed. A suite of statistical programs enables the clinician to condense, or dissect, information in order to understand better (and in a more valid manner) a mass of data which in its raw form is indigestible and confusing.

CHAPTER 8

Concluding and Reporting Your Research

STEP 7: REACH A CONCLUSION

It is necessary at this stage of your research to bring the investigation full circle, linking the results to the hypotheses (and thus the literature) so that it is clear how the hypotheses fared.

The discussion of conclusions

It is here that you explain (without repeating your results) what they mean and how they relate to other researchers' findings/-theories. After discussing the results relating to the hypotheses (i.e. whether or not the results are statistically significant) you draw out conclusions about any other statistically significant results you have obtained. Mitchell and Jolley (1988) state that if the results are as predicted, the discussion is mainly a 'reiteration of the highlights of the introduction and results sections'. If the results are unexpected the discussion section is usually an attempt to 'reconcile the introduction and results section'.

The results, of course, have to be set out as clearly as possible — the step we are coming to — and then reported succinctly. In reporting your results and conclusions, try to find that difficult balance between comprehensiveness and economy in your reporting. Also be explicit. You may know what you have in mind in discussing complex findings, but your reader won't. 'Unpack' complicated results and conclusions to make them clear.

STEP 8: SET OUT/REPORT YOUR RESULTS

Results can be presented in many different ways (Tufte, 1983). The most common are tables, histograms (Figure 9), graphs

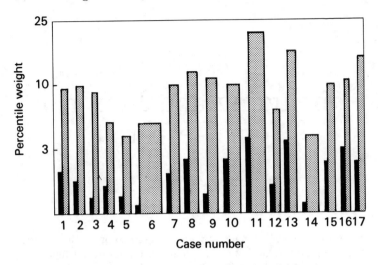

Figure 9. Change in percentile ranking (weight) between beginning and end of intervention (from Iwaniec *et al.*, 1985b)

Goal: that Mrs Hayes shall feel able to cope with her depression

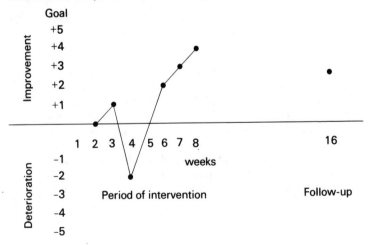

Figure 10.

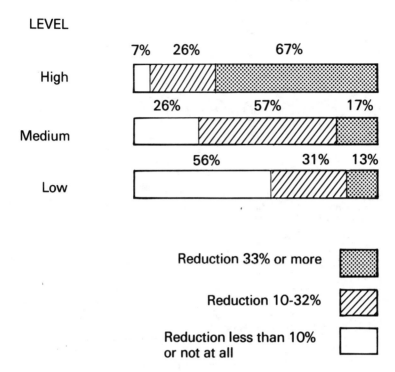

Figure 11. Relation of reduction of insomnia to three
levels/dosages of sleeping potion 'Sleepwell' (this is an
imaginary record for illustrative purposes)

(Figure 10), bar charts (Figure 11), and illustrations (Figure 12),
respectively. Sometimes, if the data warrant it, a case study
reporting method can be used to present data (Herbert, 1987a,
b).

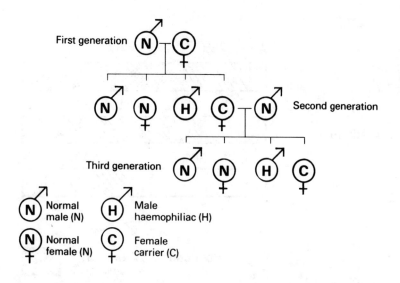

Note: The genetic possibility of sons inheriting haemophilia from a carrier mother, and daughters being carriers is roughly 50 per cent. However, in reality this pattern can vary.

Figure 12. Inheriting haemophilia through three generations

Writing up your research

Try to keep your report uncluttered by using appendices for material (data, illustrations, examples, etc.) that is of interest, but not salient to the main thrust of the exposition. Be clear in your mind about your 'audience' — who you are writing for. What is it you wish to communicate? A critique is in order; also a comment on what you might have done with the 'wisdom of hindsight'. Does your research generate new ideas for further research or suggest the modification of a current theory? Keep the discussion as concise and pertinent as possible.

While trying to organize and edit material into a manageable paper or dissertation, imagine that a serious radio science programme's interviewer has asked you to explain to the listeners (fairly briefly) *what* you have been investigating, *why*, *how*, and with what results. Such a mental rehearsal will concentrate your mind and help you tease out the nub of the work you are going to elaborate in your report. It will also provide you with the essentials for the obligatory *abstract*.

It leads on to an important early step in report writing: the *outline*. The following outline provides you with headings (and comment) in an order which will give your report coherence and clarity (see also Appendix IV).

Title (preferably not in excess of 15 words)

Keep it concise and self-explanatory. The *keywords* which give readers/literature searchers access to your work should indicate the theoretical and/or practice issue(s) to which your research is addressed, plus the dependent and independent variable(s) studied.

Abstract (100–175 words)

Once again, try to keep it concise and self-explanatory. It should include:

1. The main hypotheses, e.g. the prediction that treatment X will cause an effect Y.
2. A synopsis of the methods used.
3. A summary of the major findings.
4. A brief mention of subjects and materials.
5. The conclusions based on the results.
6. Experimental design procedures.

Introduction

Sternberg (1977) suggests setting yourself four questions to answer in this section:

1. What previous research led to your research project?
2. What does your study add to this previous research?
3. Why is such an addition important or interesting?
4. How is the addition made?

Papers written for refereed journals include a *brief, critical* review (see Light and Pillemer, 1984, on reviewing research). Theses usually require a more 'leisurely' and extensive overview of the literature; it is expected to be scholarly, often touching on the historical/philosophical background to the issues under investigation. Do not neglect to cite reports that go against your hypothesis. Too often such reviews are descriptive, not analytical, uncritical rather than critical (see Haywood and Wragg, 1982, on evaluating the literature). Check that your citations are accurate and not surplus to requirement.

Hypotheses

Set these out clearly. Make sure they are explicit and are derived correctly from the theory, if you have cited one. Explain the rationale for the selection of *methods*; is it derived logically from the hypothesis?

Method

In this section you explain in detail the what, *why* and how of the procedures you used in order to generate the data. The ground rule is to describe your method in sufficient detail to allow the reader to replicate your study precisely should he or she so wish — without personal access to you for supplementary detail. Your subheadings might take the following form, although not necessarily in this order:

1. *Materials*: a description, with (if appropriate) illustrations/ examples.
2. *Apparatus*: a description, drawing or photograph.
3. *Subjects*:
   - Total number participating in the study (sample size).
   - The number receiving each 'treatment' (i.e. experimental condition) (subsample sizes).
   - The population from which the sample of subjects was drawn.
   - The manner in which they were drawn (e.g. randomly) from the population to which the results will be generalized.
   - The circumstances under which the subjects participated (e.g. volunteer patients, fellow students). How was informed consent obtained?
   - Sex, age, educational and other significant details. Note any possible biases in sampling (e.g. high refusal rates, institutional setting).
4. *Research design*: includes a description of:
   - The experimental group(s).
   - The control/contrast group(s).
   - The manner in which subjects are assigned to groups.
   - The independent variable(s) ⎰ and how they are to
   - The dependent variable(s) ⎱ be measured
   - A specification of which variables are between-subjects and which are within-subjects.

Where measures are fully described elsewhere, it is usually sufficient to provide a concise summary description, but always accompanied by a reference. Give fuller details if measures are of your own devising. Provide information

about their psychometric properties, e.g. reliability and validity. Also include examples in an appendix.
5. *Procedure*: includes a chronological account of what happens to the subjects in the experimental sessions from first contact to the end of the study. Include instructions/directions to subjects. When you have used more than one measure, report whether the order of administration was counterbalanced, and effects analysed statistically.

Results

Set out your findings incorporating the major results in tables and figures as appropriate. Include the data central to your thesis in the text; consign other material to appendices. Try to avoid repetition and redundancy in your reporting as between tables and commentary (text). Try to keep the tables from being overly 'busy' and thus confusing. You might order the analysis as follows:
- descriptive statistics;
- exploratory data analysis;
- confirmatory/discomfirmatory data analysis.
Report the statistic you used to obtain p values (significance levels); use two-tailed tests, preferably, and provide sufficient information for the reader to check vital conclusions (see Appendix IV).

Discussion and conclusion

This should take you full circle, relating back to your hypotheses and the literature you reviewed.

The contents outline of a longer report (subject to the special requirements/regulations of an institution or funding body) is likely to follow a pattern like the one below:

- Title page
- Preface
- Contents
- List of tables
- List of figures
- List of other types of material

- Chapters
- Appendices
- List of references
- Bibliography
- Index
- (An abstract is always required)

It is always wise to write more than one draft of your paper. Let a little time elapse between the penultimate draft and the final one. Look at what is (hopefully) the final version with relatively 'fresh' eyes. Now ask a colleague to read it with *genuine* (!) carte blanche to write 'editorial' comments in the margin. If you don't (or can't) mean it, then don't. You might lose a friend or friendly colleague.

EPILOGUE

The write-up of a research report is the logical place to end this bird's-eye view of the research process. I hope it may now seem a less formidable activity for those who were somewhat apprehensive. Granted, there is a need for much supplementary and focused reading and consulting (where possible) of experts in particular areas. Not only is research a vital enterprise in expanding the frontiers of knowledge, but it can also be fun. I mentioned Brooks and Watts (undated) in an earlier part of the book, and I'd like to return to them to end with. They bemoan the fact that far too many projects treat research and data analysis 'as some mechanical series of computations rather than an interesting "detective story", involving identifying sources of variation within their data; identifying trends, etc. which had not been predicted but which may well be of clinical interest'.

These comments seem to have taken us full circle to the Preface, in which Kerlinger put in a plea for intuition and imagination in research. I hope that that curiosity that makes 'detectives' of those of us who study psychology or who practise in the helping professions will also serve us well as researchers. Serendipity — accidental discovery — is part of the fun and excitement of doing research.

Preparing a Research Proposal

(see also Howard and Sharp, 1983)

AIMS

To develop a realistic plan of action (blueprint) for your proposed research project.

ACTION

Prepare your proposal and submit it in writing (keep it as brief as possible! This helps concentrate the mind).

1. Prepare a synoptic analysis of the topic (three or four A4 pages of type). Cover the following ground:
   (a) prior research in your area;
   (b) its value;
   (c) questions it raises for you;
   (d) methodology (if any) it suggests to you.
2. Prepare your research proposal (length depends on setting for presentation and/or audience, say funding committee). Cover the following ground:
   (a) summary;
   (b) the major *questions* you are asking;
   (c) hypotheses or research objectives;
   (d) value in terms of possible outcomes (the 'so what?' question discussed on page 7);
   (e) probable methodology or approach to the research;
   (f) tentative schedule (logistics of seeking permission from ethical committee; making preliminary arrangements for getting subjects; timetable for testing/interviewing; analysing data; writing up; typing, etc.);
   (g) provisional contents outline (e.g. sections/chapters).
3. Provide details of estimated costs.

APPENDIX II

A Student Research Proposal

(reproduced with permission)

Research Proposal: Mark Gresswell
(first draft)   Department of Psychology.

Title   *Explanations of offending and their
            relationship to service delivery in a
            Special Hospital.*

Proposer: Mark Gresswell, Probationer Clinical
            Psychologist. Research undertaken for
            third-year Course in Clinical Psychology
            leading to the award of an MSc.

Clinical Supervisor:

Academic Supervisor:

Introduction/Aims:
Many explanations of offending behaviour have been advanced
by academics covering a wide range of factors and models.
Explanations for criminality are also held by the lay public,
where they have been found to be multi-dimensional
(Furnham and Henderson, 1983). Although work has been done
to examine the explanations of offending held by some
professionals and how these explanations could affect attitudes
to victims, management of offenders etc., no work has yet
been undertaken where explanations of offending held by
special hospital staff have been examined and related to
service delivery.

The majority of the work in this field has focused on
explanations of crime and how these vary with demographic
differences in respondents. However, a study by Cann *et al.*
(1980) has shown that the systematic manipulation of

information presented to respondents about the offender and the nature of his offence can elicit different explanations which will have implications for how the offender would be managed. Sex offending, for example, is often associated with mental instability (Hollin and Howells, 1987).

The aim of this research is to examine the explanations held by a group of staff at the hospital for offending behaviour and investigate how these vary when descriptions of offence behaviour and psychiatric label are manipulated. These explanations should be open to comparison with those offered by the lay public, and an attempt will be made to see how they affect expectations for service delivery.

This research is worth attempting because of the implications that explanations have for patient care and referral to psychology and other disciplines, staff allocation, patient allocation and, indeed, for the increased understanding of hospital dynamics.

Design:

A brief patient history will be created using the same format as that found on the 'short history sheet' at the front of each patient's file. From this one basic description six variations will be made differing only in one or two sentences. These differences will involve two *offence behaviours* and three *hints at psychiatric labels* as indicated below:

| | EXPERIMENTAL CONDITIONS | | |
| | (six variations) | | |
Label/hint	Psychosis	Psychopathy	Mental handicap
Offence			
Sexual assault	1	2	3
Non-sexual assault	4	5	6

Each subject will be given one description to read and will then be asked to rate the imaginary patient on the following scales:

1. Most likely diagnosis (free choice).
2. Questionnaire based on Furnham and Henderson (1983) and modified down to 18 items by Hollin and Howells (1987). Subjects will be required to rate 18 explanations on seven-point scales according to how appropriate they think the explanations are of the offending behaviour.

3. Which professional could offer the best overall assessment.
4. Which professional could offer the best assessment regarding managing the patient on the ward.
5. Best treatment option.
6. Estimated length of stay at hospital.
7. Long-term prognosis:
   (a) disposal;
   (b) treatment outcome/psychiatric problems;
   (c) recidivism.

Staff will also be asked to indicate their profession and length of service at the hospital. These procedures could be undertaken by staff either at home or at their place of work and would take an estimated maximum of 30 minutes to complete.

Subjects:
It is estimated that a minimum of 60 subjects will be required, 10 per group. (Obtaining and testing this number could prove a difficulty and negotiations with nursing staff are in progress.) To eliminate as many confounding variables as possible it would be best if the subjects were drawn from the male nurse population; they would be randomly assigned to experimental conditions.

Analysis:
Analysis should be possible via six 2×2 ANOVAs crossing 'offence' with 'label' variables. The 18-item questionnaire should be amenable to factor analysis.

References:
Cann, A., Calboun, L. G., and Selby, J. W. (1980). Attributions of delinquent behaviour: Impact of consensus and consistency of information. *British Journal of Social and Clinical Psychology*, **19**, 33–46.

Furnham, A., and Henderson, M. (1983). Lay theories of delinquency. *European Journal of Social Psychology*, **13**, 107–120.

Hollin, C. R., and Howells, K. (1987). Lay explanations of delinquency: Global or offence-specific. *British Journal of Social Psychology*, **26**, 203–210.

American Psychological Association's Principles Governing the Treatment of Human Participants

A. In planning a study, the investigator has the responsibility to make a careful evaluation of its ethical acceptability. To the extent that the weighing of scientific and human values suggests a compromise of any principle, the investigator incurs correspondingly serious obligation to seek ethical advice and to observe stringent safeguards to protect the rights of human participants.

B. Considering whether a participant in a planned study will be a 'subject at risk' or a 'subject at minimal risk', according to recognized standards, is of primary ethical concern to the investigator.

C. The investigator always retains the responsibility of ensuring ethical practice in research. The investigator is also responsible for the ethical treatment of research participants by collaborators, assistants, students and employees, all of whom, however, incur similar obligations.

D. Except in minimal-risk research, the investigator establishes a clear and fair agreement with research participants, prior to their participation, that clarifies the obligations and responsibilities of each. The investigator has the obligation to honour all promises and commitments included in that agreement. The investigator informs the participants of all aspects of the research that might reasonably be expected to influence willingness to participate and explains all other aspects of the research about which the participants enquire. Failure to make full disclosure prior to obtaining informed consent requires additional safeguards to protect the welfare and dignity of the research participants. Research with children or with participants who have impairments that would limit understanding and/or communication requires special safeguarding procedures.

E. Methodological requirements of a study may make the use of concealment or deception necessary. Before conducting such a study, the investigator has a special responsibility to (i) determine whether the use of such techniques is justified by the study's prospective scientific, educational or applied value; (ii) determine whether alternative procedures are available that do not use concealment or deception; and (iii) ensure that the participants are provided with sufficient explanation as soon as possible.

F. The investigator respects the individual's freedom to decline to participate in or to withdraw from the research at any time. The obligation to protect this freedom requires careful thought and consideration when the investigator is in a position of authority or influence over the participant. Such positions of authority include, but are not limited to, situations in which research participation is required as part of employment or in which the participant is a student, client or employee of the investigator.

G. The investigator protects the participant from physical and mental discomfort, harm and anger that may arise from research procedures. If risks of such consequences exist, the investigator informs the participant of that fact. Research procedures likely to cause serious or lasting harm to a participant are not used unless the failure to use these procedures might expose the participant to risk of greater harm, or unless the research has great potential benefit and fully informed and voluntary consent is obtained from each participant. The participant should be informed of procedures for contacting the investigator within a reasonable time period following participation should stress, potential harm or related questions or concerns arise.

H. After the data are collected the investigator provides the participant with information about the nature of the study and attempts to remove any misconceptions that may have arisen. Where scientific or humane values justify delaying or withholding this information, the investigator incurs a special responsibility to monitor the research and to ensure that there are no damaging consequences for the participant.

I. Where research procedures result in undesirable consequences for the individual participant, the investigator has the responsibility to detect and remove or correct these consequences, including long-term effects.

J. Information obtained about a research participant during the course of an investigation is confidential unless otherwise agreed upon in advance. When the possibility exists that others may obtain access to such information, this possibility, together with the plans for protecting confidentiality, is explained to the participant as part of the procedure for obtaining informed consent.

Note. From *American Psychologist* (1981), **36**, 633–638. Copyright by the American Psychological Association. Reprinted by permission.

A Reader's, Writer's and Reviewer's Guide to Assessing Research Reports in Clinical Psychology*

Brendan A. Maher
Harvard University

The editors of the *Journal of Consulting and Clinical Psychology* who served between 1974 and 1978 have seen some 3500 manuscripts in the area of consulting and clinical psychology. Working with this number of manuscripts has made it possible to formulate a set of general guidelines that may be helpful in the assessment of research reports. Originally developed by and for journal reviewers, the guidelines are necessarily skeletal and summary and omit many methodological concerns. They do, however, address the methodological concerns that have proved to be significant in a substantial number of cases. In response to a number of requests, the guidelines are being made available here.

TOPIC CONTENT

1. Is the article appropriate to this journal? Does it fall within the boundaries mandated in the masthead description?

STYLE

1. Does the manuscript conform to APA style in its major aspects?

---

* These guidelines could well apply to other helping professions, e.g. social workers, psychiatry, medicine (author's comment).

INTRODUCTION

1. Is the introduction as brief as possible given the topic of the article?
2. Are all of the citations correct and necessary, or is there padding? Are important citations missing? Has the author been careful to cite prior reports contrary to the current hypothesis?
3. Is there an explicit hypothesis?
4. Has the *origin* of the hypothesis been made explicit?
5. Was the hypothesis *correctly* derived from the theory that has been cited? Are other, contrary hypotheses compatible with the same theory?
6. Is there an explicit rationale for the selection of measures, and was it derived logically from the hypothesis?

METHOD

1. Is the method so described that replication is possible without further information?
2. Subjects: were they sampled randomly from the population to which the results will be generalized?
3. Under what circumstances was informed consent obtained?
4. Are there probable biases in sampling (e.g. volunteers, high refusal rates, institution population atypical for the country at large, etc.)?
5. What was the 'set' given to subjects? Was there deception? Was there control for experimenter influence and expectancy effects?
6. How were subjects debriefed?
7. Were subjects (patients) led to believe that they were receiving 'treatment'?
8. Were there special variables affecting the subjects, such as medication, fatigue, and threat that were not part of the experimental manipulation? In clinical samples, was 'organicity' measured and/or eliminated?
9. Controls: were there appropriate control groups? What was being controlled for?
10. When more than one measure was used, was the order counterbalanced? If so, were order effects actually analysed statistically?
11. Was there a control task(s) to confirm specificity of results?
12. Measures: for both dependent and independent variable measures — was validity and reliability established and reported? When a measure is tailor-made for a study, this is very important. When validities and reliabilities are already available in the literature, it is less important.

13. Is there adequate description of tasks, materials, apparatus, and so forth?
14. Is there discriminant validity of the measures?
15. Are distributions of scores on measures typical of scores that have been reported for similar samples in previous literature?
16. Are measures free from biases such as:
    (a) Social desirability?
    (b) Yeasaying and naysaying?
    (c) Correlations with general responsivity?
    (d) Verbal ability, intelligence?
17. If measures are scored by observers using categories or codes, what is the inter-rater reliability?
18. Was administration and scoring of the measures done blind?
19. If short versions, foreign-language translations, and so forth, of common measures are used, has the validity and reliability of these been established?
20. In correlational designs, do the two measures have theoretical and/or methodological independence?

REPRESENTATIVE DESIGN

1. When the stimulus is a human (e.g. in clinical judgements of clients of differing race, sex, etc.), is there a *sample* of stimuli (e.g. more than one client of each race or each sex)?
2. When only one stimulus or a few human stimuli were used, was an adequate explanation of the failure to sample given?

STATISTICS

1. Were the statistics used with appropriate assumptions fulfilled by the data (e.g. normalcy of distributions for parametric techniques)? Where necessary, have scores been transformed appropriately?
2. Were tests of significance properly used and reported? For example, did the author use the p value of a correlation to justify conclusions when the actual size of the correlation suggests little common variance between two measures?
3. Have statistical significance levels been accompanied by an analysis of practical significance levels?
4. Has the author considered the effects of a limited range of scores, and so forth, in using correlations?
5. Is the basic statistical strategy that of a 'fishing expedition'; that is, if many comparisons are made, were the obtained significance levels predicted in advance? Consider the

number of significance levels as a function of the total number of comparisons made.

FACTOR ANALYTIC STATISTICS

1. Have the correlation and factor matrices been made available to the reviewers and to the readers through the National Auxiliary Publications Service or other methods?
2. Is it stated what was used for communalities and is the choice appropriate? Ones in the diagonals are especially undesirable when items were correlated as the variables.
3. Is the method of termination of factor extraction stated, and is it appropriate in this case?
4. Is the method of factor rotation stated, and is it appropriate in this case?
5. If items are used as variables, what are the proportions of yes and no responses for each variable?
6. Is the sample size given, and is it adequate?
7. Are there evidences of distortion in the final solution, such as single factors, excessively high communalities, obliqueness when an orthogonal solution is used, linearly dependent variables, or too many complex variables? Are artificial factors evident because of inclusion of variables in the analysis that are alternate forms of each other?

FIGURES AND TABLES

1. Are the figures and tables (a) necessary and (b) self-explanatory? Large tables of non-significant differences, for example, should be eliminated if the few obtained significances can be reported in a sentence or two in the text. Could several tables be combined into a smaller number?
2. Are the axes of figures identified clearly?
3. Do graphs correspond logically to the textual argument of the article? (e.g. if the text states that a certain technique leads to an *increment* of mental health and the accompanying graph shows a *decline* in symptoms, the point is not as clear to the reader as it would be if the text or the graph were amended to achieve visual and verbal congruence.)

DISCUSSION AND CONCLUSION

1. Is the discussion properly confined to the findings or is it digressive, including new post hoc speculation?
2. Has the author explicitly considered and discussed viable alternative explanations of the findings?

3. Have non-significant trends in the data been promoted to 'findings'?
4. Are the limits of the generalizations possible from the data made clear? Has the author identified his/her own methodological difficulties in the study?
5. Has the author 'accepted' the null hypothesis?
6. Has the author considered the possible methodological bases for discrepancies between the results reported and other findings in the literature?

(This material may be reproduced in whole or in part without permission, provided that acknowledgement is made to Brendan A. Maher and the American Psychological Association.)

APPENDIX V

Guide to a Library Search

- *Psychological Abstracts:* these deal with specific years or half-years of psychological publications, printing the abstracts/summaries which head most journal articles. They list the source, the title and the author/s' affiliations. The issues come in two parts:
1. The *index*, which lists subjects and authors and gives a code number for the relevant abstract. You start with the index to find the abstracts you need, then go to the appropriate catalogue.
2. The *catalogue* lists the abstracts by code number.

- *The Psychological Thesaurus* tells you other subject titles under which your criterion variable might be listed (the concept 'self' is also referred to as identity, personality and ego). Once you have found your criterion variable you turn to the abstracts.

- *Current Contents:* these are published in sections and consist of the *contents pages* of journals which have recently appeared. Authors' addresses are also printed so you can request a reprint of the article if the title seems relevant (see Sternberg, 1977, for a detailed list of important psychological journals).

- *Exerpta Medica* and *Index Medicus* are useful medical abstracting journals.

- *Social Sciences Index* is a comprehensive source for journal references in all the social sciences, e.g. sociology, social work, psychology, anthropology and geography. Each index entry takes the following form: title, author, brief description, journal, volume, number, pages, month, year.

- *Social Science Citation Index* indexes articles that appear in over 2000 journals; it includes a subject index, source (author) index and a citation index.

• *The Citation Index* gives a specific reference (say a paper on sex education for mentally handicapped adolescents by Brown and Smith, 1979). You have heard of it and if you look up in the index you will find there the authors who have cited this paper and whose work may therefore be of interest to you.

REFERENCES

Allport, G. (1937). *Psychology of personality*. London: Constable.

Anastasi, A. (1982). *Psychological testing* (5th edn). New York: Collins-Macmillan.

Bakan, D. (1967). *On method: A reconstruction of psychological investigation*. New York: Jossey-Bass.

Bakeman, R., and Gottman, J. M. (1986). *Observing interaction: An introduction to sequential analysis*. Cambridge: Cambridge University Press.

Bannister, D., and Fransella, F. (1980). *Inquiring man* (2nd edn). Harmondsworth: Penguin.

Barber, T. X. (1976). *Pitfalls in human research: Ten pivotal points*. New York: Pergamon.

Barlow, D. H., and Hayes, S. C. (1979). Alternating treatments design. *Journal of Applied Behavior Analysis*, **12**, 199–210.

Barlow, D. H., Hayes, S. C., and Nelson, R. O. (1984). *The scientist practitioner: Research and accountability in clinical and educational settings*. New York: Pergamon.

Bellack, A. S., and Hersen, M. (Eds) (1984). *Research methods in clinical psychology*. Oxford: Pergamon.

Berger, M. (1980). *Research projects: A guide for students*. Department of Child Development and Educational Psychology, University of London Institute of Education.

Borchardt, D. H., and Francis, R. D. (1986). *How to find out in psychology*. Oxford: Pergamon.

Bromley, D. E. (1977). *Personality description in ordinary language*. Chichester: Wiley.

Bromley, D. E. (1986). *The case-study method in psychology and related disciplines*. Chichester: Wiley.

Brooks, D. N., and Watts, F. N. (undated manuscript). Comments on research dissertations submitted for the B.P.S. Diploma in Clinical Psychology. Leicester: British Psychological Society.

Brown, G. W., and Harris, T. O. (1978). *Social origins of depression: A study of psychiatric disorder in women*. London: Tavistock.

Brown, S., and McIntyre, D. (1981). An action-research approach to innovation in centralized educational systems. *European Journal of Science Education*, **3**, 243–258.

Browne, K. (1986). Methods and approaches to the study of

parenting. In W. Sluckin and M. Herbert (Eds), *Parental behaviour*. Oxford: Blackwell.

Bulmer, M. (1982). *Social research ethics*. London: Macmillan.

Buros, O. (Ed.) (1978). *The eighth mental measurements year book*. Lincoln: University of Nebraska/Gryphon Press.

Camilli, G., and Hopkins, K. D. (1978). Applicability of chi-square to 2 × 2 contingency tables with small expected cell frequencies. *Psychological Bulletin*, 85, 163–167.

Campbell, D. T., and Stanley, J. C. (1966). *Experimental and quasi-experimental designs for research*. Chicago: Rand McNally.

Campbell, J. P., Daft, R. L., and Hulin, C. L. (1982). *What to study: Generating and developing research questions*. Beverly Hills: Sage Publications.

Child, I. L. (1973). *Humanistic psychology and the research tradition*. New York: Wiley.

Cohen, J. (1977). *Statistical power analysis for the behavioural sciences*. New York: Academic Press.

Cook, T. D., and Campbell, D. T. (1979). *Quasi-experimentation: Design and analysis issues for field settings*. Chicago: Rand McNally.

Cronbach, L. J., and Gleser, G. C. (1965). *Psychological tests and personnel decisions*. Urbana: University of Illinois Press.

Durlak, J. (1979). Comparative effectiveness of paraprofessional and professional helpers. *Psychological Bulletin*, 86, 80–82.

Ferguson, G. A. (1966). *Statistical analysis in psychology and education* (2nd edn). New York: McGraw-Hill.

Flanagan, J. C. (1954). The critical incident technique. *Psychological Bulletin*, 51, 327–358.

Gould, S. J. (1981). *The mismeasure of man*. Harmondsworth: Penguin.

Graham, H. (1986). *The human face of psychology*. Milton Keynes: The Open University Press.

Gurman, A. S., and Kniskern, D. P. (1978). Research in marital and family therapy. In S. Garfield and A. E. Bergin (Eds), *Handbook of psychotherapy and behavior change*. New York: Wiley.

Hardiker, P., and Littlewood, J. (1987). *Guidelines for dissertations* (2nd edn). University of Leicester School of Social Work and Loughborough University of Technology Department of Social Science.

Harris, R. J. (1985). *A primer of multivariate statistics*. New York: Academic Press.

Hartwig, F., and Dearing, B. E. (1980). *Exploratory data analysis*. London: Sage.

Hayes, S. C. (1981). Single case experimental design and empirical clinical practice. *Journal of Consulting and Clinical Psychology*, **49**, 193–211.

Hays, W. L. (1981). *Statistics for the social sciences* (3rd edn). New York: Holt, Rinehart & Winston.

Haywood, P., and Wragg, E. C. (1982). *Evaluating the literature.* Rediguide 2, University of Nottingham, School of Education.

Herbert, M. (1964). The concept and testing of brain-damage in children: A review. *Journal of Child Psychology and Psychiatry*, **5**, 197–216.

Herbert, M. (1987a). *Behavioural treatment of children with problems: A practice manual.* London: Academic Press.

Herbert, M. (1987b). *Conduct disorders of childhood and adolescence: A social learning perspective* (2nd edn). Chichester: Wiley.

Herbert, M., Sluckin, W., and Sluckin, A. (1983). Mother-to-infant 'bonding'. *Journal of Child Psychology and Psychiatry*, **23**, 205–221.

Holsti, O. R. (1969). *Content analysis for the social sciences and the humanities.* Reading, MA: Addison-Wesley.

Howard, K., and Sharp, K. (1983). *The management of a student research project.* Aldershot: Gower.

Howell, D. C. (1982). *Statistical methods for psychology.* Boston: Duxbury.

Huff, D. (1954). *How to lie with statistics.* New York: Norton.

Iwaniec, D., Herbert, M., and McNeish, A. S. (1985a, b). Social work with failure-to-thrive children and their families. *British Journal of Social Work*, **15**, (a) Part 1: Psychosocial factors, 243–259; (b) Behavioural social work intervention, 375–389.

Jehu, D. (1972). *Research methods.* Unpublished paper, School of Social Work, University of Leicester.

Johnson, J. M., and Pennypacker, H. S. (1980). *Strategies and tactics of human behavioural research.* Hillsdale, NJ: Lawrence Erlbaum.

Judd, C. M., and Kenny, D. A. (1981). *Estimating the effects of social intervention.* Cambridge: Cambridge University Press.

Kay, H. (1978). Preface. In J. Radford and D. Rose (Eds), *The teaching of psychology.* Chichester: Wiley.

Kazdin, A. E. (1982). *Single case research designs.* Oxford: Oxford University Press.

Kerlinger, F. N. (1986). *Foundations of behavioural research.* New York: Holt, Rinehart & Winston.

Kessel, F. S. (1969). The philosophy of science as proclaimed and science as practised: 'Identity' or 'dualism?' *American Psychologist*, **24**, 999–1005.

Kuhn, L. T. S. (1970). Reflections on my critics. In I. Lakatos and

A. Musgrave (Eds), *Criticism and the growth of knowledge.* Cambridge: Cambridge University Press.

Lee, S. G., and Herbert, M. (1970). *Freud and psychology.* Harmondsworth: Penguin.

Leighton, A. H. (1979). Research directions in psychiatry epidemiology. *Psychological Medicine,* 9, 234–247.

Light, R. J., and Pillemer, D. P. (1984). *Summing up: The science of reviewing research.* Cambridge, MA: Harvard University Press.

Marascuillo, L. A., and McSweeney, M. (1977). *Nonparametric and distribution-free methods for the social sciences.* Monterey, CA: Brooks Cole.

Martin, P., and Bateson, P. (1987). *Measuring behaviour.* Cambridge: Cambridge University Press.

Masters, W. H., and Johnson, V. (1970). *Human sexual inadequacy.* Boston: Little, Brown.

Mausner, J. R., and Kramer, S. (1985). *Epidemiology, an introductory text.* Philadelphia: Saunders.

Maxwell, A. E. (1958). *Experimental design in psychology and the medical sciences.* London: Methuen.

Miller, C. (1983). Guidelines and notes on method for a project/-Evaluation research methods — A guide. In *Research and projects from a workshop.* London: CCETSW Study 6.

Mitchell, M., and Jolley, J. (1988). *Research design explained.* London: Holt, Rinehart & Winston.

Parkes, C. M. (1980). Bereavement counselling: Does it work? *British Medical Journal,* 5 July.

Parlett, M., and Dearden, A. (Eds) (1977). *Introduction to illuminative evaluation.* California: Pacific Soundings Press.

Parlett, M., and Hamilton, D. (1978). *Evaluation as illumination: A new approach to the study of innovatory programmes.* Occasional Paper No. 9, Centre for Research in the Educational Science, University of Edinburgh.

Schiffman, S. S., Reynolds, M. L., and Young, F. W. (1981). *Introduction to multidimensional scaling: Theory, methods and applications.* New York: Academic Press.

Siegel, B. (1956). *Non-parametric statistics for the behavioural sciences.* New York: McGraw-Hill.

Som, R. K. (1973). *A manual of sampling techniques.* London: Heinemann.

Sternberg, R. J. (1977). *Writing the psychology paper.* New York: Barron's Educational Series.

Sutton, C. (1987). *A handbook of research for the helping professions.* London: Routledge & Kegan Paul.

Toch, H. (1969). *Violent men.* Chicago: Aldine.

Truax, C., and Carkhuff, R. (1967). *Towards effective counselling and psychotherapy*. Chicago: Aldine.

Tufte, E. R. (1983). *The visual display of quantitative information*. Cheshire, CN: Graphics Press.

Tukey, J. W. (1977). *Exploratory data analysis*. Reading, MA: Addison Wesley.

Whyte, W. F. (1981). *Street corner society* (3rd edn). Chicago: Chicago University Press.

Young, P. V. (1966). *Scientific social surveys and research*. New York: Prentice-Hall.

TECHNICAL BIBLIOGRAPHY

I METHODS

Aitken, L. R. (1985). *Psychological testing and assessments* (5th edn). Boston: Allyn & Bacon.

Berdie, D. R., and Anderson, J. F. (1974). *Questionnaires: Design and use*. Metuchen, NJ: Scarecrow Press.

Brenner, M. (Ed.) (1985). *The research interview: Uses and approaches*. London: Academic Press.

Burgess, R. C. (1982). *In the field: An introduction to field research*. London: George Allen & Unwin.

Fransella, F., and Bannister, D. (1977). *A manual for repertory grid technique*. London: Academic Press.

Glaser, B. G., and Strauss, A. L. (1967). *The discovery of grounded theory: Strategies for qualitative research*. London: Weidenfeld & Nicolson.

Gordon, R. L. (1969). *Interviewing strategy: Techniques and tactics*. Homewood, IL: Dorsey Press.

Maanen, J. Van (Ed.) (1983). *Qualitative methodology*. Beverley Hills: Sage.

McCall, G. J., and Simmons, J. L. (1969). *Issues in participant observation: A textbook and reader*. Reading, MA: Addison-Wesley.

Marsh, C. (1982). *The survey method*. London: George Allen & Unwin.

Miles, M. B., and Humberman, A. M. (1984). *Qualitative data analysis: A sourcebook of new methods*. London: Sage.

Moser, C., and Kalton, G. (1971). *Survey methods in social investigation* (rev. edn). London: Heinemann.

Neale, J. M., and Liebert, R. M. (1986). *Science and behaviour: An introduction to methods of research* (3rd edn). Englewood Cliffs, NJ: Prentice-Hall.

Oppenheim, A. N. (1966). *Questionnaire design and attitude measurement*. London: Heinemann.

Patton, M. Q. (1980). *Qualitative evaluation methods*. Beverly Hills: Sage.

Plummer, K. (1984). *Documents of Life*. London: George Allen & Unwin.

Slade, P. D. (1982). Towards a functional analysis of anorexia nervosa and bulimia nervosa. *British Journal of Clinical Psychology*, **21**, 167–179.

Spradley, J. P. (1980). *Participant observation*. New York: Holt, Rinehart & Winston.

Stone, P. J., Dunphy, D. C., Smith, M. S., and Ogilvie, D. M. (1966). *The general inquirer: A computer approach to content analysis*. Cambridge, MA: MIT Press.

Sudman, S., and Bradburn, N. M. (1982). *Asking questions: A practical guide to questionnaire design*. San Francisco: Jossey-Bass.

Walker, R. (Ed.) (1985). *Applied qualitative research*. Aldershot: Gower.

Webb, E. J. *et al.* (1966). *Unobtrusive methods: Nonreactive research in the social sciences*. Chicago: Rand McNally.

Yin, R. K. (1984). *Case study research*. Beverly Hills: Sage.

II OUTCOME RESEARCH (EVALUATION)

Meta-analysis

(the method of aggregating detailed summaries of psychotherapy controlled outcome studies and teasing out the 'effects')

Journal of Consulting and Clinical Psychology (1983), **51**. (The February 1983 issue contains an invited section on meta-analysis).

Smith, M. L., Glass, V. V., and Miller, J. T. I. (1980). *The benefits of psychotherapy*. Baltimore: Johns Hopkins.

General Studies

Barlow, D. H., and Hersen, M. (Eds) (1984). *Single-case experimental designs* (2nd edn). Oxford: Pergamon.

Bergin, A. E., and Garfield, S. L. (Eds) (1971). *Handbook of psychotherapy and behaviour change*. New York: Wiley.

Bloom, M., and Fischer, J, (1982). *Evaluating practice: A guide for professionals*. Englewood Cliffs, NJ: Prentice Hall.

Garfield, S. L. (1981). Psychotherapy: A 40-year appraisal? *American Psychologist*, **2**, 174–183.

Goldberg, E. M., and Connelly, N. (Eds) (1981). *Evaluative research in social care*. London: Heinemann.

Gurman, E. M., and Razin, A. M. (1977). *Effective psychotherapy: A handbook of research*. New York: Pergamon.

Kazdin, A. E. (1986). Comparative outcome studies of psychotherapy: Methodological issues and strategies. *Journal of Consulting and Clinical Psychology*, **54**, 95–105.

Kazdin, A. E., and Wilson, G. T. (1978). *Evaluation of behavior therapy: Issues, evidence and research strategies.* Cambridge, MA: Ballinger.

Mitchell, K. M., Bozarth, J. D., and Krauft, C. C. (1977). A reappraisal of the therapeutic effectiveness of accurate empathy, nonpossessive warmth and genuineness. In Gurman and Razin (1977).

Rachman, S. J., and Wilson, G. T. (1980). *The effects of psychological therapy.* (2nd edn). Oxford: Pergamon.

Waskow, I., and Parloff, M. (1975). *Psychotherapy change measures.* Washington, DC: US Government Printing Office.

Weiss, C. (1972). *Evaluation research.* Englewood Cliffs, NJ: Prentice-Hall.

III STATISTICAL ANALYSIS

Anderberg, M. R. (1973). *Cluster analysis for applications.* New York: Academic Press.

Batchelor, B. G. (1978). *Pattern recognition.* New York: Plenum Press.

Box, G. E. P., and Jenkins, G. M. (1976). *Time series analysis.* San Francisco: Holden-Day.

Chatfield, C., and Collins, A. J. (1980). *Introduction to multivariate analysis.* London: Chapman & Hall.

Child, D. (1970). *The essentials of factor anlaysis.* London: Holt, Rinehart & Winston.

Everett, B. S. (1980). *Cluster analysis.* (2nd edn). London: Heinemann.

Lockyer, K. G. (1969) *An introduction to critical path analysis.* (3rd edn). London: Pitman.

Lovie, A. D. (Ed.) (1986). *New developments in statistics for the social sciences.* London: Methuen/British Psychological Society.

Moser, C. A., and Kalton, G. (1971). *Survey methods in social investigation.* (2nd edn). London: Heinemann.

Plewis, I. (1985). *Analysing change.* Chichester: Wiley.

Singer, B. (1970). *Distribution-free methods for non-parametric problems.* Leicester: British Psychological Society.

IV REPORT WRITING

Day, R. A. (1979). *How to write and publish a scientific paper.* Philadelphia: ISI Press.

O'Connor, M., and Woodford, F. P. (1978). *Writing scientific papers in English.* Tunbridge Wells: Pitman Medical Publishing.

Sternberg, R. J. (1977). *Writing the psychology paper.* New York: Barron's Educational Series.

V THE USE OF COMPUTERS

Brownell, B. A. (1985). *Using microcomputers: A guide book for writers, teachers and researchers.* Beverly Hills: Sage.

Norris, D. E., Skilbeck, C. E., Hayward, A. E., and Torpy, D. M. (1985). *Microcomputers in clinical practice.* Chichester: Wiley.

Norusis, M. J. (1983). *SPSS-X Introductory Statistics Guide.* New York: McGraw-Hill.

Norusis, M. J. (1985). *SPSS-X Advanced Statistics Guide.* New York: McGraw-Hill.

Schrodt, P. A. *Microcomputer methods for social scientists.* Sage University Paper Series on Quantitative Applications in the Social Sciences, series no. 07–040. Beverly Hills: Sage.

SPSS Inc. (1983). *SPSS-X User's Guide.* New York: McGraw-Hill.

Standing Committee on Test Standards. Note on the computerization of printed psychological tests and questionnaires (1984). *Bulletin of the British Psychological Society,* 37, 416–417.

VI APPLYING FOR GRANTS

Bellack, A. S., and Hersen, M. (Eds) (1984). *Research methods in clinical psychology.* Oxford: Pergamon.

Burcham, W. E., and Rutherford, R. J. D. (1985). Writing applications for research grants. Educational Development Advisory Committee Occasional Publication No. 3. University of Birmingham.

FURTHER READING

Bell, J. (1987). *Doing your research project: A guide for first-time researchers in education and social science.* Milton Keynes: Open University Press.
A source of reference and good practice for beginners in the educational and social science fields.

Bellack, A. S., and Hersen, M. (Eds) (1984) *Research methods in clinical psychology.* Oxford: Pergamon.
This is an excellent guide, not only for clinical psychologists, but anyone in the helping professions interested in doing research or being sophisticated about evaluating the research of others.

Borchardt, D. H., and Francis, R. D. (1984). *How to find out in psychology: A guide to the literature and methods of research.* Oxford: Pergamon.
This is an invaluable book which provides an annotated survey of the literature of psychology and its methodology — and is thus of relevance to professionals (from various disciplines) in their practice and research activities.

Burgess, R. G. (1982). *Field research: A sourcebook and field manual.* London: George Allen & Unwin.
A useful guide to field research methodology.

Edwards, A. (1969). *Statistical analysis.* (3rd edn). New York: Holt, Rinehart & Winston.
A good book for the beginner.

Hays, W. (1981). *Statistics.* (3rd edn). New York: Holt, Rinehart & Winston.
A more advanced text, research orientated, one of the best guides available.

Howard, K., and Sharp, J. A. (1983). *The management of a student research project.* Aldershot: Gower.
A practical guide that caters for up to doctoral level of research.

Judd, C. M., and Kenny, D. A. (1981). *Estimating the effects of social interventions.* Cambridge: Cambridge University Press.
A comprehensive introduction to methods for measuring the impact of social interventions, including mental health programmes, child-care centres, educational projects, etc.

Kazdin, A. E. (1982). *Single case research designs.* Oxford: Oxford University Press.

An overview of the methodology much used by behaviour therapists and behavioural counsellors.

Kerlinger, F. N. (1986). *Foundations of behavioral research.* (3rd edn). New York: Holt, Rinehart & Winston.
A superb book covering every aspect of research, with *examples* of the different types available to you (drawn from actual published studies).

Mitchell, M., and Jolley, J. (1988). *Research design explained.* New York: Holt, Rinehart & Winston.
This is a very useful introductory guide because of its extensive range, helpful illustrations and clear explanations.

Phillips, E. M., and Pugh, D. S. (1987). *How to get a Ph.D.* Milton Keynes: Open University Press.
Indispensable to the postgraduate threading his or her lonely route through the 'minefield' of doctoral research.

Reason, P., and Rowan, J. (Eds) (1981). *Human inquiry: A sourcebook of new paradigm research.* Chichester: Wiley.
Several valuable contributions, but note J. Heron on experimental research.

Silvey, J. (1975). *Deciphering data.* London: Longman.
A guide to the processes involved in analysing a social survey; helpful in coding, SPSS, path analysis, patterning of responses, and many other subjects.

Sternberg, R. J. (1988) *The psychologist's companion.* Cambridge: Cambridge University Press/British Psychological Society.
An updated version of Sternberg (1977) (listed on p. 118) with excellent additional material on (*inter alia*) graphing, tabulating and setting out, by other means, your data.

Sutton, C. (1987). *A handbook of research for the helping professions.* London: Routledge & Kegan Paul.
A bird's-eye view of the variety and range of important empirical research in areas of interest and value to people in the helping professions.

Truax, C., and Carkhuff, R. (1967). *Towards effective counselling and psychotherapy.* Chicago: Aldine.
A must for counsellor practitioners and researchers.

NAME INDEX

SUBJECT INDEX